Generous

Generous

Marcus Armytage

Foreword and
breeding appendix by
Tony Morris

MARLBOROUGH/PUNCHESTOWN

AUTHORS AND PUBLISHERS THANKS

Both the author and the publisher would like to express their thanks to the many people and organisations who made this book possible and would particularly like to mention Prince Fahd and Anthony Penfold and their secretarial staff; Paul and Venessa Cole and all at Whatcombe; Generous' jockeys, Alan Munro and Richard Quinn; David and Diane Nagle and their staff at Barronstown Stud; Tim Corballis and Christy Grassick at Coolmore and everyone else there; Philip Myerscough and Nick Nugent and all at Goffs Sales at Kill; Hamish and Belinda Alexander and their staff at Partridge Close Stud and the hundreds of other people who helped.

We must express particular thanks to Michael Harris, Brough Scott and *The Racing Post* for allowing us to use copyright material which had previously appeared in their paper.

CONTENTS

*Captions for illustrations are found on
pages 16, 52, 88 and 124*

MARLBOROUGH BOOKS
6 Milton Road, Swindon, SN1 5JG
c/o 9 Queen Street, Melbourne 3000, Victoria, Australia

PUNCHESTOWN BOOKS
Ormond Court, 11 Ormond Quay, Dublin 1

First published 1991
A limited edition of 75 signed and specially bound copies is
published by
The Marlborough Bookshop and Sporting Gallery

Typesetting and Origination Footnote Graphics, Warminster.

Jacket Design *Ron Stephens*.

ISBN 1–873919–03–4 Marlborough
ISBN 1–873920–01–6 Punchestown

Printed in Great Britain by
Billings and Sons Limited, Worcester

FOREWORD

GENEROUS restored some of the old virtues and values to racing in an age when dull conformity, specialisation and fear of defeat have become the negative norm. Boldly campaigned over a wide range of distances, always in the best of company, he displayed a degree of versatility unmatched by lesser so-called champions of modern times.

This is his story, the story of a proper racehorse, vividly portrayed by a comparably versatile young man, as accomplished with the pen as in the saddle.

Tony Morris

IRISH BEGINNINGS

The flight from Cape Town, South Africa to Buenos Aires, Argentina is a long one. The party of five, David and Diane Nagle, owners of Barronstown Stud at Grange Con in Ireland, Terence Millard, champion trainer of South Africa, Laurie Jaffee and Des Scott, both leading owners in that country, remember this particular trip well. The South Africans because they bought an Argentinian yearling, Prontissimo, that went on to become a champion racehorse in their country and the Nagles because, as a direct result of this trip, they bought a broodmare called Doff The Derby. For the purposes of the Generous story, this flight, struck by enormous good fortune, is where it all began.

David Nagle, as a director and auctioneer of Goffs, had travelled the world with his gavel and his gift of the gab. He had sold in many parts of the world and in one year sold the highest priced yearlings on three different continents. However most of all he enjoyed his winter contracts auctioneering in South Africa and hence his friendship with Terence, Laurie and Des.

As already mentioned the flight from Cape Town to Buenos Aires is a long, tedious one and it was Laurie who was up and down the aisles entertaining the others. Having been away from home for a fortnight David and Diane had not seen a racing paper or magazine for some time but as luck would have it Laurie had a copy of the *American Bloodhorse* with him which he gave to Diane to read.

"But for Laurie I doubt we would ever have bought Doff The Derby," she says now looking back at that moment.

9

For tucked away in a quarter-page corner of the *Bloodhorse* was the report of an obscure bloodstock sale in California.

"I noticed," she recalled, "that a good friend of ours, Melinda Smith, had bought an unraced half-sister to Trillion, the Champion older mare in Europe in 1977. We also knew that David O'Brien, Vincent's son, had a very good two-year-old in training out of Trillion called Tryptych. I pointed out the article to David."

Their journey took in several studs in Argentina en route for the Rio Carnival in Brazil while thoughts of purchasing Doff The Derby were put on the back-burner. "It is a hell of party, I'd recommend it to anyone," says David, "and we hired Ronnie Biggs as our guide! I don't think that the establishment would have appreciated it but he looked after us well and I see he now advertises himself as a guide."

The next stage of their journey took them to The Bahamas where they were due to meet John Magnier and John Horgan. John Magnier is part-owner of Coolmore Stud and a partner in all the Nagle's bloodstock. As David puts it so succinctly: "He owns half of almost everything we've got, unfortunately we don't own half of everything he's got!" The pair met at school and have remained great friends and business partners ever since. John Horgan, another friend from Ireland, owned the 1990 Two Thousand Guineas winner Tirol.

It was in The Bahamas that the purchase of Doff The Derby was taken beyond the it's-a-nice-thought stage. Indeed in Argentina and then Brazil they had not been in much of a position to do anything about it. Diane mentioned the article to John Magnier who was keen to do something about it. After several phonecalls to Kentucky the deal for the mare was struck.

The year was 1985, Doff The Derby was four and Melinda, as David recalls with a smile but without mentioning figures, drove a hard bargain considering the length of time the mare had been hers.

Diane Nagle is the daughter of that great Irish trainer Paddy Sleator. From Grange Con, the same village whose links with racing are continued through Barronstown Stud, Paddy Sleator dominated Irish steeplechasing with fellow trainer Tom Dreaper for many years. Paddy, now in his 80s still resides in the village which is situated half an hour from The Curragh on the border between counties Wicklow and Kildare.

Paddy, who trained amongst others Another Flash who won the 1960 Champion Hurdle and Scottish Memories who won the 1961 Mackeson Gold Cup, was an innovative trainer. He was ahead of his time. He bought up a mile stretch of the local railway when it closed down and by laying down cinders along it is credited with the construction of the first ever all-weather gallop. He also used to send some of his best jumpers to run in England. They were 'officially' trained by Arthur Thomas at Warwick although Paddy did all their entries and it was his lads who looked after the horses. However, the Jockey Club frowned upon this and, in order to combat the raids, eventually took Thomas' licence away.

David Nagle married Diane in 1975 having met her while auctioneering in South Africa the year before. With swept back hair, like many compatriots of the same ilk, he seems to have life well and truly sorted for his family. They are good-fun people and between them they haven't half had some good times when horses have been added to the equation.

David's father was a lawyer who hunted and although there was no direct family link with horseracing he was always around the animals. David's own passion for foxhunting developed at an early age.

As an auctioneer for Goffs he was asked by South African breeders to conduct their Johannesburg Sales in

11

1975. For 15 years he had travelled the world selling horses from Sydney to San Francisco. All in all he sold horses in 13 different countries but his greatest feat, as a non-French speaker, was to persuade the French that their pre-Arc de Triomphe Sale, such an international affair as it was, should be conducted in English, selling in dollars.

Then, of course, came those records when the smooth talking auctioneer knocked down the highest priced yearlings on three different continents in the year of his marriage, Ir 127,000 gns in Ireland, 55,000 rand in South Africa and $50,000 in Australia. "It was nothing to do with me," he recalls. "The market was just taking off and I just stood there hollering."

When he finished with Goffs, he and Diane settled down to make Barronstown the stud that it is today. In between they have had considerable sport with the odd jumpers that they have owned in partnership with friends. In particular they enjoyed notable success with Attitude Adjuster, named after a cocktail found at McCarthy's Bar in Fethard. He won the Christies Foxhunters at Cheltenham and ran in the Grand National several times always giving them a good run for their money. They also had a share in the ill-fated Kingsmill, winner of the Irish Champion Hurdle. Indeed they make no bones about the fact that they would sooner own a jumper than a flat horse despite the latter being the commodity that earns them a living.

Now that Barronstown is established David has taken up the Mastership of the Duhallow Hounds who hunt in the South of Ireland on the Cork–Limerick border. The sport is good and wild down there, it is one of the few places of which you could genuinely say that the quality of their hunting has not been affected by 20th century farming practices.

But at the beginning of the Eighties Grange Con was in danger of being written off the racing map altogether.

Small Grange Con is not the prettiest of villages although it is situated in an undulating landscape with the Wicklow Hills away off in the distance in an easterly direction. Dublin is an hour's drive away. Paddy Sleator had just retired and the Nagles, at this stage, were only just beginning to put the stud together. Indeed when they sold foals in 1980 they did not have the cheek to call themselves a stud and sold under the name of friend and neighbour Johnny Harrington's Commonstown Stud. Barronstown consists of about 500 acres of pasture. It is made up of its own 250 acres which surround the house, 100 acres rented from Paddy Sleator and another 100 or so acres rented from another farm. It was originally founded on two gift horses, one called Golden Hind came from Mick Rogers, who in Hard Ridden (1958) and Santa Claus (1964) is the only Irishman other than Vincent O'Brien to have trained more than one Epsom Derby winner. She had been barren for a while before arriving but produced four super foals in succession at Barronstown. The other was Winfield Lily who was a similar success.

The need for a quick turnover at this early stage in the stud's development meant that the off-spring were sold as foals rather than as yearlings. They still sell half of their foals.

"We are what you might call 'getting-out' traders," says David. "The only way we got into the business was by getting rid of them. We were lucky with Golden Hind though, she produced good looking stock and we learned at an early stage that it was more important to have a good looker than a good pedigree."

But we return to the arrival of Doff The Derby in 1985, the mare bought on a whim who, by the time her third foal had completed the High Summer Treble, was probably the most valuable broodmare in Europe.

"When we got her back, not having seen the sale catalogue we were unaware that she had been covered as a two-year-old and that she had already had a yearling by the American stallion Jaklin Klugman. She waddled like a duck and had never raced.''

The waddle and the fact that she had never raced was the result of a fracture, not as one might immediately suppose to her leg, but to her tail. History doesn't relate how she broke it but, as Ned Gowing, a vet from The Curragh and a great family friend of the Nagles confirms, when a horse breaks its tail it is often near its coccyx and the bones do not always realign as they should afterwards. The galloping horse needs its tail for balance and therefore steering, a bit like a cat does for walking along the top of a wall or a boat needs its rudder. With a crooked tail there was no chance of her making it as a racehorse, indeed if it makes her waddle at the walk, what would it do to her at the gallop?

Doff The Derby is a bay mare with two white heels behind, a white near-hind hoof and has a white star on her forehead with a white nose. She stands at 15.3 hh. She was by Master Derby out of a good old mare called Margarethen who was 19 when she produced Doff The Derby. Margarethen was a tough individual having won 16 races in the States including a Grade 3 Handicap. Just short of really top class she was placed in 13 other races including Grade 2 handicaps.

''It was a nice surprise when we found out that she had foaled Windy Triple K, a filly by Californian Derby winner Jaklin Klugman,'' remembers David, ''especially as the filly went on to win five races there.'' Rarely can a modern Derby-winner producing mare have foaled at three.

''Initially we sent her to Alleged in America but it was a late covering and she didn't take so we brought her back here and sent her to Kings Lake the following season,'' recalls Diane.

Her second foal, the first in Ireland, was by Kings Lake. Named Wedding Bouquet she was trained by Vincent

O'Brien and owned by his wife Jacqueline. She would already be showing her potential on the track as a two-year-old when Generous was coming up for sale as a yearling.

The third foal was Generous, the result of the mating with Caerleon. The choice of Caerleon as a stallion was principally at the behest of John Magnier, a partner in the mare and as already mentioned a major shareholder in Coolmore Stud, the 3,000 acre thoroughbred breeding establishment in which he, Robert Sangster and Vincent O'Brien have invested so heavily in recent years.

Coolmore is situated a mile outside the Tipperary town of Fethard. By English standards Fethard is little more than a village made up of a main highstreet, a handful of shops, the famous McCarthy's bar and, of course, a betting shop. There is no racecourse here but it is a popular racing area.

Few smallholdings are without a stable tucked away at the back of the garden housing a hunter or a potential Cheltenham Gold Cup winner being prepared for its first bumper. Always 'for sale' at 'the right price,' these horses often raise a tidy sum to supplement agriculture through hard times. Few children grow to a school-leaving age here without having handled horses or ponies in one shape or form; most are competent horsemen before they even get to go to school.

If you drive through this part of Ireland you get a wonderful feeling that you're travelling through a land forgotten by time, small fields, sagging wooden gates hanging at awkward angles to their hinges, cableless tractors, dairy cattle wandering out to grass after milking. There is an Irish rural charm about the Tipperary countryside. Sign posts, where they haven't been removed or pointed in the wrong direction by local children, are in imperial and metric distances alternatively. Between them they confuse one's sense of distance and direction.

PHOTOGRAPH CAPTIONS
PAGES 17–20

Page 17

Top – Generous was foaled at the famous Coolmore Stud in County Tipperary. It is not only one of the great thoroughbred breeding establishments of the world but also a beautiful estate as can be seen from this photograph. Generous' sire, Caerleon is a permanent resident there.
Bottom – A polaroid picture taken when Generous was only a few hours old for identification purposes. Certainly the earliest picture of a Derby winner ever published in a book.

Page 18

Top – This picture shows the modern stud buildings of Barronstown Stud owned by David and Diane Nagle in County Wicklow. Like Coolmore, Barronstown is a world famous name in breeding circles and year after year its consignments of foals and yearlings to the major sales at nearby Goffs at Kill and Tattersalls are eagerly inspected by owners, bloodstock agents and trainers.
Bottom – A typical paddock at Barronstown where Generous was to spend the summer and early autumn months of his first year.

Page 19

Top – Generous was bought by Hamish Alexander of the Partridge Close Stud and he is seen here talking to his head man Derek Guy.
Bottom – Generous in his yearling days, playing in one of Hamish's paddocks.

Page 20

Robert Latham who looked after Generous throughout his racing career.

However as you approach Coolmore from Fethard you immediately get the feeling that the place is more business-like. Smartly painted blue gates announce your presence on the estate. You are following a giant Brown-built six-horse box. Decked out in the Coolmore colours it is one of the five owned by the stud. It is totally out of proportion to the 25-year-old tractor you just overtook down the road.

As business goes anywhere, let alone in this part of the world, horsebreeding at Coolmore is big. During the foaling season they will employ 150 people including the management, vets, stud hands, farm staff, gardeners, maintenance men and students.

It was originally a small country stud owned by blood-stock agent Tim Vigors who now operates out of New-market. The limestone based land, so beneficial to the consistent production of healthy stock, has a great history for producing both flat and jumping winners.

Three Grand National winners were bred here and the winners of eight Cheltenham Gold Cups. It was home to some of the great chasing sires, Fortina, Cottage, Even Money and Deep Run. The present owners have developed it into one of the most successful studs in the world with stallions either bred or bought by the partner-ship. Although it is now very much geared towards breeding for the valuable flat market, everyone is catered for from the small local farmer with one jumping mare upwards.

Foaling units, isolation boxes and barns are scattered about the estate and are connected by a network of private roads. The place is kept immaculately tidy, buildings are well designed, light, airy, functional, roomy and com-fortable with an obvious quality about them. In recent years the place has become a showpiece for visiting foreign diplomats.

As a stud Coolmore can now boast the greatest con-centration of Northern Dancer's blood – racing's single most influential sire this century – anywhere in the world.

Caerleon had been high up in the stallion lists from day one, his first crop of three-year-olds made him Champion sire in 1988 but the result of his meeting with Doff The Derby was to seal his reputation as a stallion. The winner of the 1983 French Derby and by Nijinsky, Caerleon was tough as a racehorse rarely plagued by unsoundness and, as you might expect of a grandson of Northern Dancer, has a high fertility rate.

Christy Grassick, manager of the stud, describes Caerleon simply as 'uncomplicated'. He suggests that this was the magic gene passed on with such success by Northern Dancer. When a stud deals with the number of horses that Coolmore does, it can cope with difficult horses but so much better an uncomplicated stallion.

Following the arrival of Doff The Derby's Kings Lake foal, Wedding Bouquet in 1987, the mare remained with her foal at Coolmore until she had been served and confirmed pregnant to Caerleon. Her last service date with Caerleon was 1st March of that year. Once confirmed she returned to Barronstown with her foal. There she remained until 23rd December, when with Christmas approaching and heavily in foal, she travelled back down to Coolmore to prepare for the birth of her third offspring.

There are a number of foaling barns at Coolmore and Doff The Derby was assigned to and installed in the Springhill Unit. The mares in this particular barn are the stud's own, in other words belonging to any of the partners, and are therefore kept separate from visiting mares to minimise any risks of disease. There are 24 boxes here, a dozen either side of a main pasage with an exit to a covered woodchip ring where mares can be teased and foals exercised.

As the mare was due to foal early she went immediately into her foaling box on arrival. Had she been later she would have waited in another barn until a Springhill box had become available nearer the time.

Three hundred or more foals will be delivered safely into the world in an average season at Coolmore but, even by their standards, the night of 8th February 1988 was a busy one; a Sadler's Wells filly, two Thatching foals, a Glenstal, a Glow, a Kings Lake, a Bering and the Caerleon colt. Doff The Derby was one of eight to foal down that evening. By 8.30 pm she had, after a simple birth, produced a healthy chestnut colt. Generous, like the seven others that night, had slipped quietly into the world in an uncomplicated, unspectacular fashion under the warming glow of a heat lamp. No problems, no need for the vet to be called out – he was not on special duty like he would have been had Doff The Derby been an old mare which case there would have been a greater likelihood of her haemorrhaging. The nightman on duty that evening would have been able to mutter to himself how he wished all foalings at Springhill were as simple as this one.

Within an hour Generous, no bigger than an Irish wolfhound and weighing 118 lb, was up and suckling at the rich and vital colostrum provided by his dam. There was no way this strong little foal was going to be what Coolmore describe as an 'off-sucker', one that refuses to go to the milk-bar. Those are the nightmen's nightmares because it means they have to spend most of the night hand milking the mare as you would a cow.

Doff The Derby and the chestnut foal remained at Springhill for five days. The birth-giving process is exhausting for both mother and 'child'. That first night they are both routinely checked for any abnormalities. It is also normal for the foal to be given an enema to relieve any pressure that may have built up in his bowels during the birth.

Having strengthened up during the night, his first day at Coolmore was a busy one. It is not dissimilar to the routine a child goes through on its arrival at a busy maternity ward, particularly that morning.

As already mentioned about 300 foals will arrive at Coolmore through the season. For one of these to stand out from that crowd, there has to be something spectacular about it or something drastically wrong with it. Generous, as a newly arrived foal, was described by Christy as a 'straightforward bloke'.

That morning after was purely routine as far as Generous was concerned. The mare and her foal were moved to a fresh box comfortably bedded with home-produced wheat straw.

Each foal, already the proud wearer of a brand new headcollar with his sire and dam inscribed upon it, is checked for broken ribs that may have been cracked during the birth-giving process. It is not an uncommon injury associated with foaling. Generous, like the other seven born that night, would have been laid on his back while a stud hand checked and felt each rib individually. A blood sample would also have been taken for analysis in Coolmore's own high-tech laboratory.

For the stud records a foaling report is made by the foaling manager, in Generous's case by Joe Foley and by a vet, John Halley M.R.C.V.S. From Coolmore's point of view this is an important procedure ensuring any conformation problems are spotted at an early stage. A polaroid photo is taken of the 12-hour-old foal and he is weighed, in this case, at 118 lbs. The mare's placenta is also weighed, Doff The Derby's being an average 15 lb.

The foaling comment reads: No difficulties.

The vet's comment reads: Good size and strength but weak colour.

Vet and foaling manager discuss a general score for the foal's overall conformation. Generous achieved a rating of 7.5 out of a possible 10. This system is Coolmore's own and the ratings are revised and rechecked each month.

"Seven and a half is a well-above average score," says Christy Grassick. "Eight is very good, an outstanding foal, and means, on looks, that you have a star. You will see very few eight and a halves in a lifetime, so Generous was not far off being one of the best looking foals we had around that year.

"We find that the score may fluctuate during the year when they are growing but we nearly always find that when they are yearlings they are back to that original first rating which makes it an important inspection."

"Weak colour." Until Generous had won the Derby some three years and four months later his colour, chestnut with a flaxen mane and multicoloured tail, had the same effect on potential purchasers that a white question mark painted on to his backside would have done. Experienced horsemen, although taken by his breeding and conformation, were time and time again to write him off because of it. Perhaps they had forgotten Grundy but had Generous been born a simple bay, he may never have ended up where he did. The horse himself was not likely to know the significance of his colour so why a chestnut with a flaxen mane and tale remains such a subject of superstition among trainers and owners remains a mystery.

On 9th February 1988 Generous was a pale milky chestnut. "Their colour at birth is not always indicative of their eventual colour which usually deepens until they are yearlings," says Christy. "Some people give them seaweed to help this process if they are a bit pale and wishy-washy like Generous but I personally don't think it makes a lot of difference.

"Other than his colour there was no particular reason to remember him while he was here," he adds. "He was never sick and he had a good temperament. We'd be telling fibs if we could tell you that he did anything wrong."

On day five Generous was wormed for the first time,

25

receiving paste orally, and then again at monthly intervals. The same day he and Doff The Derby were moved to a new barn to make way for another expectant mare at Springhill. They moved up to the Sadler's Wells barn where they could be turned out every day. On a cold or wet day it might only be for 20 minutes, longer if it was finer, but Coolmore believes in getting its foals out, they have eventually to be prepared for a competitive world, and that competitive world might as well start here in one of the foal paddocks. Whether a potential Classic winner or a potential nonentity, they all get treated alike at this stud.

Generous, healthy and good natured, spent the remainder of his time at Coolmore, his owners and the owners of the stud unaware that in just over three years time they would be offering big money for his return there as a stallion. He and Doff The Derby remained in the rolling Tipperary countryside until 3rd May that year when the pair made the hour and a half journey north to Grange Con. For the mare, who had been covered by Sadler's Wells, it was going home, for Generous, it was a new home.

Trainers, stud owners, even Pony Club mothers with their children's 12.2 hh pony will confirm that when it comes to equine health, if it is catchable, horses will catch it.

Diane Nagle is unable to trace Generous's veterinary record for his time as foal back at Barronstown. "It is not because we are inefficient," she says. "It is because our vet Ned Gowing never had to look at him and consequently a veterinary record was never made out for him."

Gowing, whose practice looks after a large number of The Curragh's bloodstock, confirms the fact. "Apart from admiring him in the paddock, I was never called out to specially look at him."

David Nagle has his theories on the difference a clean bill of health throughout his racing career made to the horse. "To be as healthy as Generous has been through-out, not only his time here but with Hamish Alexander and Paul Cole, must make the difference between a horse being top class and a champion, especially in this day and age when a yard rarely seems to get through a season without picking up one virus or another. Here alone his health would have allowed him to grow stronger and develop better than a sickly foal. It must be a major contributory factor to his success."

Little was to ever upset Generous as a foal either. He was regularly wormed and did not mind it. His feet were occasionally rasped by the farrier and he was constantly being checked over by the Nagles. Nothing bothered him.

On 27th June 1988, aged four and a half months, he was weaned from Doff The Derby. It was the day after Kahyasi had completed the Epsom–Irish Derby double just up the road at The Curragh. Neither mare nor foal shed any tears.

The policy at Barronstown is to give the foals as much room as they can possibly want. Three or four to a fourteen acre paddock, each with an open-sided barn for cover and an old coloured hunter to nanny them. The weaning is staggered so that not all four foals lose their 'mums' the same day.

"We try to stick to nature as best we can, that is why we don't overstock the place. We give them the best hay and oats and they are out most of the time. They may look a bit hairier than other people's at the sales but that doesn't matter. We certainly wouldn't entertain the idea of rugg-ing them up like they do out in Kentucky," says David.

There was never any question as to what age Generous should remain at Grange Con. "We often sell them as foals because of the need for turnover in the early days."

Generous was subsequently entered for the Goff's December Foal Sale. He was assigned a lot number of 349 and three weeks before he was due to be sold, his preparation began.

Preparing a foal for sale is something akin to preparing a yearling for sale only on a much smaller scale. A yearling may be walked for an hour a day for seven weeks before he comes under the hammer. Foals at Barronstown are walked short distances for about 21 days.

And so the first chapter of Generous' life drew to close when he set off for Kill, an hour away in the horse box where he had been allotted a stable, Box 17 in Barn O.

A YEAR IN DURHAM

Denys Smith's smart new horsebox wound its way along the A1 back towards County Durham. The journey from Stansted Airport had been a long one, worsened by the road's permanent state of disrepair. Past Doncaster, further on to Darlington where it turned off on to the A68 for West Auckland and on to the wilder fringes of Durham.

The box, with its two equine passengers, Generous and a Petorius colt subsequently named Persuasius, passed through Tow Law, an old mining village situated on top of a long hill. It is one of those rare places where you can bump start a car on a cold morning in any direction such is its position at the crown of the hill. It is also one of those places which always smells of coal smoke, be it midwinter or high summer, although this, like the industry which has supported it for so long, is changing. A sign as you enter Tow Law now traitorously proclaims the recent connection of gas.

Here the lorry made a right turn towards Lanchester, down through Satley and past the Punch Bowl Inn, later to become the scene of some of the more riotous celebrations following Generous' great victories. The Geordie publican, Robbie Jackson, is barely understandable to untrained southern ears as he clothes and punctuates each sentence with the word: "Mun". Man.

"Noow then, mun, whatt'le y'be drinkin, mun?" An enthusiast for racing and punting, Robbie, who is built somewhat like a stone outhouse, has recently bought a horse with some of his customers. He has applied to the Jockey Club for Guinness coloured silks with a froth cap.

Right again after the village and the box swung into the yard of Partridge Close Stud which was to be Generous' home for the next 11 months.

Since 1968 it has been the property of Hamish Alexander to whom the Caerleon colt had been knocked down at the Goff's Cartier Million Sale at Kill for Ir 80,000 gns a couple of days previously.

Now you might think at this stage that the yearling had, as he travelled by Bishop Auckland, passed the last outpost of thoroughbred civilisation into a region haunted by nothing save ghostly pit-ponies and old hunters and where the only organised racing is for whippets and pigeons. But Bishop Auckland is where Arthur Stephenson regularly trains a hundred jump winners a year and it is also where Denys Smith, owner of the horsebox, has trained with success under both codes for many years.

But, let's face it, long cold winters and with Hexham, on the side of a bleak hill as the nearest racecourse, we are not talking Newmarket or for that matter Barronstown from whence Generous had arrived. The silver spoon with which he was born had, it must have seemed momentarily to the colt, been traded for a wooden one.

That is not to say Partridge Close is scruffy. Far from it. A collection of beef cattle, fowl and dogs reassure homesick yearlings on their arrival that they have joined one big happy family.

But as areas go County Durham is not the most fashionable or famous for the breed. It is, however, not without a prestigious racing history although it would be a very ancient Briton who could claim to remember the good old days.

Spilletta, dam of the immortal Eclipse, was bred at Windlestone, a couple of miles from Partridge Close, by Sir Robert Eden Voltigeur, after whom the York mile and a half Group 2 race for three-year-old colts is named, was bred in the county at the Hart Stud. During the early part

30

of the last century the Croft Stud, near Darlington, was the then equivalent of the present Dalham Hall set-up, standing some of the country's finer stallions.

Nearby Neasham Hall Stud achieved a notable feat when breeding Kettledrum and Dundee, first and second respectively in the 1861 Derby. Seven years later the same stud was responsible for Formosa, winner of the One Thousand Guineas, Two Thousand Guineas, The Oaks and St Leger. And besides producing iron and steel, the Consett Ironworks were equally famous in the 1850s for being the birthplace of Underhand, who appropriately won the Northumberland Plate, otherwise known as the Pitman's Derby.

However for the best part of a century, but for some useful steeplechasers, there had been a dearth of racing heroes to emerge from the county. In 1968 that fact did not, however, put off a freshfaced teenager, Hamish Alexander, from buying at a cost of £9,000, the derelict farmhouse, a cottage and the 100 acres that made up Partridge Close Farm.

The purchase of the land represented a considerable change in direction for Hamish. His Scottish grandfather had emigrated to Canada and his Canadian father, James, had returned with something of the entrepreneurial spirit now inherited by his son, to set up a plastics factory. During World War II the factory switched to making munitions. Afterwards substantial advantages and incentives were made available to such businesses if they relocated away from the capital so that they might bring employment back to the bombed-out hearts of other towns. Thus encouraged James Alexander moved his plastics factory to Newcastle and the family of four children, including Hamish, were brought up at Sandoe Hall.

James Alexander had more than a passing interest in racehorses and flirted with ownership.

31

Hamish recalls: "He had many fine looking staying chasers bought for him that couldn't get out of their own way. He didn't know much about the buying of horses so he went out and bought the ugliest horse he could find at one sale. He then got some friends involved and they jointly owned this horse while he ran over hurdles. They decided to sell him when he went chasing." That horse turned out to be the 1968 Grand National winner, Red Alligator, the sale of which left James Alexander more than a little miffed.

His son's prep school was Wester Elchies on the River Spey and it was there that he developed a passion for fishing. Many early morning cold showers and long distance runs later, Hamish emerged from Gordonstoun ready to try his hand as an art student at Edinburgh Art College. With long hair, more than a passing resemblence to and a certain brotherly affinity for other hippies of the Sixties, the 'youth' was indirectly being encouraged to work with horses. In his father's eyes Hamish was striding, not very purposefully, down the wrong road. He would sooner his son worked with anything but art and the druggy culture that went with it at the time.

"After a year at college I realised that there were plenty of people who could paint a lot better than me," says the former artist. "At school I had been about the best but here I would be sketching a model and would look over to the little girl next to me and notice that she was four times better. I was never going to get to that standard." The year spent at Edinburgh Art College is one he now likes to put down to experience.

At the relatively tender age of 18, by buying Partridge Close, Hamish had boldly set out with the intention of breeding thoroughbreds.

"Every penny I had was tied up in the stud and you have never seen such a dump as this place was when I bought it," he remembers.

However, although he wanted to breed a few horses, it was not quite as simple as that. He first had to earn a crust to pay for the improvements to the buildings and farm before he could begin to afford to start a breeding operation and, with the intention of killing two birds with one stone, earning a penny or two and learning about the trade, he went to Dublin.

In working for the late Nat Galway-Greer he could not have chosen a better tutor. Oxford, Cambridge, and Edinburgh Art College for that matter, weren't a patch on Galway-Greer. A doyen of his trade, what he did not know about horses, whether they be show-hunters or blue-blooded racehorses, was not worth knowing. A consistent winner at the prestigious Dublin Show, he had also had countless young potential chasers through his hands including the great Golden Miller.

"In order to earn a few quid and get a quicker turnover so that I could eventually buy the odd mare, I had to get a few foals cheaply and sell them on as yearlings, hopefully at some profit. From a financial point-of-view it was the only way I could do it," he remembers.

A successful 'pinhooker' as this type of trader or dealer, one who buys foals and sells them as yearlings, has come to be called, needs not only to be a good horseman and stockman. He also needs a good eye for a horse, knowledge of the markets, plenty of luck and some good early touches as he strives to establish himself in the business. It is a form of gambling and, at the top end of the market, the stakes can be high.

Twenty-two years after the initial success Partridge Close has earned one of the finest reputations for yearling turnouts at the sales, wherever Hamish has chosen to consign, be it Newmarket, Doncaster or at Kill in Ireland. He in turn has constantly reinvested his profits in the stud and in more foals.

"When I started there weren't many doing it and having

33

worked in Ireland with Nat I realised what a difference there was between a well turned out, well handled horse and one that had been largely ignored and unprepared. In the sales ring the difference was translated into cash. What I am doing, by taking a foal and keeping it until it is ready to go into training as a yearling approaching two, takes the bother and risk away from the eventual owner of that racehorse who may not want or have the facilities to raise the foal into a yearling."

But there are times when a pinhooker can be caught out. When the market price of yearlings almost halved between 1989 and 1990 it was the studs and people who had bought expensive foals who had to carry the can. A yearling that may have been realistically worth 100,000 gns might now fetch 45,000 gns. That said, though, pinhookers had had it pretty good during the Eighties as the introduction of Arab owners seeking to build up bloodstock empires pushed prices beyond even the most optimistic vendor's dreams.

Constant success, such as that enjoyed by Hamish Alexander, relies on something more than luck although he is the first to admit that it plays a major role. In the faded yellow press cuttings of his scrap book the word 'shrewd' keeps reappearing. Foals he bought for 200 gns were selling a year later for 9,000 gns. In 1976 three yearlings he bought for a total of 2,700 gns made 18,900 gns. "I thought at the time I'd never have to speak to my bank manager again, but I have been doing so ever since. However when you raise the game to 60,000 gns they do take you a bit more seriously!"

These are the touches you need though. It is not money for old rope. And for every good sale he makes there will be those yearlings who barely pay their way for a year's stay at Partridge Close. It is not something a doctor would advise for the faint-hearted.

Another early touch revolved around Ryan Price's 1979

Coventry Stakes winner Varingo. A year before his success Richmond trainer and friend Bill Watts had suggested to Hamish that he get hold of the half-brother foal to his most promising two-year-old, a colt called North. Watts was confident that North, who had been catching pigeons at home, would be a world-beater. Hamish was interested to know just what had happened to the yearling between North and the foal he was about to buy. "Timmy Hyde's Cammas Park Stud had sold him to Ryan Price but he's a great big thing. I wouldn't take any notice of him," confided Bill. So Hamish, on Watts's kindly advice, and quite pleased with himself thinking he had been a bit sharp on this deal, bought the foal for 5,600 gns on the strength of what North was about to do.

Sometime later Bill rang to apologise, the flying North was not fulfilling his promise and was turning out to be a big disappointment. He was sorry for letting Hamish down with such poor advice. The following summer, the very reason Hamish nearly hadn't bought the foal turned out to be Varingo. The 'great big thing' beat 17 rivals to win the Coventry Stakes at Royal Ascot. In a paddock at Partridge Close was Varingo's full-brother about to be prepared for sale. His price had multiplied many times in a couple of minutes and when sold he made 56,000 gns.

"Everyone thought I'd been really sharp," recalls Hamish, "but I'd bought him for all the wrong reasons. You need some degree of luck!"

Of course as time has progressed the figures have got bigger: in the early Eighties a foal bought for 30,000 gns, a figure substantially higher than original value of the stud, sold for 210,000 gns.

A few foals do go the wrong way but provided the right sort of horse has been bought, a pinhooker of Hamish Alexander's calibre and experience should never find a 100,000 gns foal fetching 2,000 gns a year later. The nightmare is the serious yearling that develops a splint, a boney growth near the splint bone, in which case its value may halve.

"You get some big disappointments when some of them get on the racecourse though," he reflects. "Some you thought were lovely big horses can't get out of their way and you get some that you didn't think a lot of in the paddock here, horses you'd regretted buying and were embarrassed to sell, which go and win half a dozen decent races."

But Hamish, like the Nagles and many of those connected with Generous through his first four years, is one of those people who seems to have life sorted out. He has done well for himself and family, he's found a way of life of which many would be envious. He's never happier than when he's casting for salmon on a stretch of the River Awe in Argyllshire for which he has the fishing rights or hunting with his wife Belinda with their local pack of hounds, the Braes of Derwent. He gets to spend a lot of time with his children Martha and Archie.

It is curious that he gets as big a kick out of training a couple of 'crocked' jumpers to win at nearby Hexham under a permit as he does from watching one of his former yearlings winning a Group race at Newmarket. "I can't sleep the night before Wait You There runs. I'll probably get up at 5.00 am to check he's all right. I must be mad." It is a hobby he takes seriously.

So Generous had arrived in this picturesque valley, one of the few in the area untouched by open cast mining, to be greeted by squawking chickens and barking dogs.

His purchase from the 1988 Goffs Foal Sales had been like any other well-planned Alexander foaling purchase. "Pinhooking is a gamble but many of the risks can be minimised," he says. "I'm trying to buy a foal that will both make money for me and win races later on so that my customers will come back again."

He teams up with Newmarket based bloodstock agents

36

Alex Scrope and Margaret 'Mags' O'Toole, the latter being the daughter of well-known Irish trainer Mick O'Toole. The Goffs Foal Sales this particular year were after Newmarket's equivalent; in previous years they had been before Newmarket. Mags was going home for Christmas and drew up a short-list of foals that she knew, on breeding and looks, Hamish would be interested in. This team had been working long enough to know what was required of each other and it was indeed a short list that Mags drew up this time.

"For pedigree and thoroughness Alex and Mags are top class. They are a very, very important part of my operation," comments Hamish. "They do all the sales, they know the score and the real value of horses. Mags is the most thorough girl in the world with her old man's common sense.

"It varies each December but that year there was very little worth going to Ireland for except the Barronstown consignment. They are always top class and if anyone ever wanted to learn how to prepare horses for a sale I would advise them to get a job with the Nagles."

Alex did not travel to this sale. Mags arrived on the Friday preceding the sale. "Some horses are just not Hamish's cup of tea, they have got to have a bit of pedigree," says Mags. "It is easy to be wise now after the event but we couldn't fault Generous although his colour was not a great help. It no doubt made him cheaper, if not as a foal, as a yearling. But Hamish is a gambler and if he wants a horse he'll get it. Nevertheless 80,000 gns is a lot of money if you're buying for yourself. Looking at what was available though, I suggested he would be better off putting his eggs all in one basket and have this one at that price rather than four at 20,000 gns."

Hamish himself arrived the day before the sale began and agreed with his advisers that the Caerleon colt stood out. Prices had been higher at Newmarket and he was prepared to pay a top-whack of 100,000 gns. For besides the colt's pedigree, conformation and looks he also knew that Generous's older half-sister, a yearling by Kings Lake, had just gone into training with Vincent O'Brien and that was a good sign. If O'Brien liked the filly it was a good omen.

As it was Generous, lot 349, was knocked down to Hamish for 80,000 gns. Bobby Barry was underbidder. "But for that," reflects Hamish, "we might have got him cheaper."

Generous, by now used to being loaded and unloaded from all manner of horse transport, stepped, sprightly, off the ramp of Denys Smith's box and surveyed the scene into which he had arrived and which was to be his home for the next 11 months.

Hamish employs two full-time staff with his horses, headman Derek Guy and Pauline Sudder. A student is drafted in to help prepare horses for the sales each autumn. Derek had originally worked on a stock farm before becoming James Alexander's driver in the days of the plastics factory. Very experienced with ponies, he was a stockman of the highest order and his presence since day one has undoubtedly been a major factor in the success story that has been Partridge Close Stud. He is, in his employer's words, "worth his weight in gold".

With him and Pauline looking round the foals and yearlings Hamish can sleep peacefully at night, confident that his valuable stock is in the best hands. They are a concientious pair and both have the ability to spot a sick animal two paddocks away.

On this occasion it was Derek who was at the Caerleon foal's head as he led him down the ramp. They had decided, as was their normal rule, that Generous, the most expensive of the foals at Partridge Close, was to have Box 1 in the main yard. "We usually reserve this stable for the horse we think is best," says Hamish. When Generous won the Derby the box was being occupied by his Lomond half-brother.

Derek, knowing the colt was from Barronstown, and from his experience their foals were always beautifully mannered and handled, was not worried about him doing anything daft in the strange new surroundings.

Of all those peope who have been associated with Generous it was perhaps Derek Guy who always thought the chestnut with the flaxen mane and tail would turn out to be a bit special. Everyone hopes a young horse will develop into a champion from the day a stallion is selected for his dam but it is with hope rather than confidence that thoughts of Derbys and Cheltenham Gold Cups pass through the mind. Indeed but for this 'hope' racing would not be the sport that it is. But with Derek, however, it was slightly different. From the moment that Generous arrived at the stud, he had a soft spot for him and just assumed he would be good.

The majority of horses make an impact on a place for the wrong reasons. He's the bastard who kicked Mary, he crib bites and has taught the horse next door to do the same, he's very nervous, he's just plain awkward and the other is a bad eater. But, as had been the case at Barronstown, the Caerleon colt set an example in every respect to the point of being insignificant. He was not the sort of horse you ever had to call the vet out for. He did not, like some you could mention, go looking for trouble. Had he been a child, he could have been the boy that passed through both prep and public school without ever having to visit the headmaster's study, his homework would never have been late and he would have been made a prefect on account of his good behaviour. Good looking and in all the school teams, he might just have missed out on getting the school captaincy at this stage though, for despite his reliability and willingness to learn quickly, there was something lacking. Perhaps he was just too much of a goodie-goodie, people like a bit of a rebel, a bit of charisma, in their leaders.

"I'd like to say he got loose," says Hamish wishing that every horse that came through his hands gave him as little hassle as this one, "but we hardly knew we had him on the place.

"When he arrived in December he was in smashing condition. Some people say they can look too good and, after a sale, a lot of travelling and the move to a new place that they will only go backwards but it is rubbish. I'd sooner one arrived in his sort of condition every time."

If Generous' first part of the winter in Ireland had been mild then the second was going to be tougher as anyone who has been racing at Hexham on a cold day will confirm.

Every day he would leave the comfort and warmth of his straw-bedded box for a couple of hours to be turned out with half a dozen other foals in a muddy field, regardless of weather: wind, rain, snow, anything the elements could throw at this corner of County Durham. "It looks dreadful," says Hamish. "We have a savage winter up here but with less rain than they get in the west. It tends to be colder and crisper here which is very healthy for the horses but they will probably catch some sort of cold at some stage of their winter here.

"It is nothing too serious because it never seems to affect my jumpers but I suspect it helps toughen them up and gives them some immunity from similar ailments for the future. We have 30 horses on the place through the winter here and there just isn't time to molly-coddle them, we run a common-sense job here."

As the winter eases the foals, now yearlings, get turned out for longer periods, and when the grass begins to grow in April they will stay out day and night, initially with some extra food to set them off.

"He was a beautiful horse to look after," recalls Derek.

"A real gentleman, no malice. His younger brother, by Lomond and also owned by Fahd Salman, has the same temperament with perhaps a little more presence than Generous. You could go into his stable when he was lying down and you could sit by his shoulder and talk to him, he was very friendly."

All the while Generous and the other yearlings were being educated, not so much at this stage for the yards where they were destined to be trained, but in life. Jack and Jill, the Alexander's terriers, would wander into his box whenever the door was open for a spot of mousing, chickens would flap across the yard. Wait You There and other jumpers would be pulled out for their daily exercise, the hounds would meet round the front of the house and the children's grey 12.2 hh pony might untie itself and wander loose across the yard.

Some humans are naturally laid-back and one has to suppose Generous was born that way, but between Coolmore, Barronstown and the family farm atmosphere of Partridge Close, Generous had become almost bomb-proof and it was not until, under the stress of training and the peculiar noises of Deauville a year later that he was to crack mentally for the first and only time.

The pinhooker, having bought his foal, seen it grow through the following summer into a good looking yearling, then has to assess the situation regarding the re-sale. It is not that simple and unlike the local farmer with the 20 head of cattle, it is not necessarily prudent to load them up and take them to the nearest sale. In the case of cattle that would be Hexham, in the case of thoroughbred horses it would be Doncaster. No, Hamish has to assess where the money is going to be, which yearlings will be suited to which sale: Doncaster, Tattersalls in Newmarket, Goffs in Ireland.

"For Generous I selected Goffs at Kill. Picking the right sale can be one of the hardest things but I had always been quite lucky selling horses there and that played an important part in the decision. I sold Tocave there six years before for 210,000 gns. I'd bought him for 30,000 gns, that is what I regard as a lucky place."

Taking horses back to Ireland to sell to mainly English trainers and owners may seem an odd way of working. Hamish was one of the first to adopt the practice when the Irish punt was revalued. Now he is not alone.

The real business of preparing a yearling for sale begins in earnest seven weeks before the animal comes under the hammer. By late August or early September most of Hamish's yearlings will be back in their stables.

An attractive, well-bred yearling will attract a lot of attention at a sale. If he sells on the third day and was there two days before the sale began, then it is perfectly possible he may have been pulled out of his stable at the sales nearly 150 times, 50 times a day, before he enters the ring, by interested trainers, owners, bloodstock agents and even by semi-interested timewasters. Some will come back for a second and third look, second opinions and vets will look out for the less obvious blemishes. Therefore, no two ways about it, a yearling must be reasonably fit and well handled before he gets to the sales if he is to show himself off to the best of his ability and not to trip out of his stable with his head on the ground just because he is tired.

"Sometimes," explains Hamish, "I don't think trainers appreciate how tired these young horses get. In and out of their boxes the whole time. It is not just the physical strain either, a brainy horse would say to hell with it after a while wouldn't he? And I feel especially sorry for the fillies who might not quite have the constitution of the colts at this stage. Some people won't bring them out if they have just been fed but I'm there to sell them and if a potential buyer wants to take a look at him, I'll pull him out even if his tea has just been put in his manger."

If you are thinking ahead at this stage you may be wondering how Hamish, Derek, Pauline and a student have enough hours in the day to get nearly 30 yearlings to the level of fitness required, let alone muck them out. Here Hamish relies firmly on technology, an indoor horsewalker.

Behind the two main yards, the horsewalker is housed in a large barn and is best described as looking like a drag lift operating from the ceiling of the barn. Despite looking more in the Heath Robinson mode and somewhat older than the modern horsewalkers you now see in most training yards, it is nevertheless very reliable. The only time it ever broke down was when Hamish attached a large basket to it, loaded up Archie and Martha, and switched it to full speed. The children enjoyed the ride though.

Taking up to seven yearlings at one time, with its speed set at eight miles an hour, one circuit of the barn is roughly the equivalent of walking round the perimeter of a tennis court. Initially newcomers are introduced to it in small doses, five minutes the first day with one other horse for company. The daily amount is increased gradually until the yearling is walking briskly for an hour a day, covering eight miles. Derek stands in the centre, cajoling and encouraging his charges while Hamish and Pauline muck out their boxes.

"We don't usually get any trouble," Hamish says. "The system has worked well now for some time and it is much safer than leading yearlings up and down the lane for an hour. By the end of seven weeks the yearlings are pretty fit. I remember one time we took some horses over to Goff's in Ireland to sell. It was only the second year we had the horsewalker. They had a long journey and we decided to give them the following day off to get over the trip. I didn't realise how fit they were and when, on the second day after their arrival, we went to get them out they were so fresh we had a job controlling them. The level of fitness cannot be overstressed though, they have still got to be looking perky even when they are pulled out for the 150th time."

Generous was, as you might now expect of him, a certainty to go on that horsewalker without the slightest bother, without a moment of hesitation. That was the case. "You only ever had to show him how to do something once and he knew for next time," recalls Derek admiringly.

At evening stables the yearlings are taught to tie up, are brushed over and are left 'tied up' while Hamish, Derek and Pauline, like a triumvirate of judges at a horseshow, visit each horse in turn, pass comments, judgements and predictions and refer to the individual's progress. They were always of the opinion that Generous, still at that time referred to as the Caerleon colt, was worthy of his position in Box 1.

Vet bills for Generous's stay at the stud were, like they had been at Barronstown, almost negligible. For routine work at home Hamish uses the Stirk Brothers while at the sales he uses Peter Calver to inspect potential purchases. "Generous was very like his half-brother. When the Lomond colt had a small haemotoma on his side, the vet was able to poke around with it and he never flinched. We didn't even have to put a headcollar on him."

Of course there is a certain amount of routine veterinary work. On the first Wednesday of every month all the young bloodstock are wormed. It is a simple, uncomplicated system, easy to remember and like most things at Partridge Close based on common sense.

Apart from worming, teeth and feet are the two principal areas for attention among the yearlings. Both are checked regularly. Three weeks before the Goff's Cartier Million Sale Generous was shod for the first time. Hamish never has his yearlings shod behind, too dangerous, but

44

for the seven weeks that they have been undergoing sales preparation each yearling has had Venice turpentine rubbed into his feet on a daily basis. Horsemen in the 'old days' used Venice turpentine, more commonly used as an oil paint thickener, for curing corns in horses' feet.

Calver, who trains horses at Ripon, and is also a qualified blacksmith to boot.

"He does us proud," comments Hamish. "Nothing's complicated with Peter, no bullshit, he's a commonsense man and he vetted Generous for me when I bought him in Ireland. If he says absolutely 'no' then we don't buy it, it is as simple as that."

And so the second chapter of Generous' life was coming to an end. The hazy days of summer turned out in the paddocks of Northern England, playing with his mates, were over and life was beginning to take a turn for the more serious. The party was over.

THE MASTER OF WHATCOMBE

"NO FAHD SALMAN, NO PAUL COLE." It has been one of the trainer's favourite sayings since he and his principal owner, Prince Fahd Salman, went into partnership with Whatcombe in the mid-Eighties.

Paul Frederick Irvine Cole was born in Tonbridge on 11th September 1941. His family had been farmers from Great Somerford, near Malmesbury in Wiltshire.

His father, Harold Cole, was a major in the Wiltshire Yeomanry during the war but afterwards became an agricultural adviser for Nickersons the seed merchants. Major Cole and his wife brought up his son and daughter, Paul and Maureen, in Gillingham, not far from Wincanton Racecourse in the West Country. Maureen is now married to Stephen 'D.C.' Stanhope and lives in Ireland. Paul himself married Vanessa Ryder in 1976. The trainer's wife is a vital role in itself and Vanessa copes admirably well as housewife/hostess, entertaining owners, jollying everyone along and keeping a smile on the Guv'nor's face when things are not going smoothly.

She is a gifted cook. Although she rides a hack out most days, knows all the horses and regularly attends the big meetings and sales, she takes a mainly non-active role in the day-to-day running of the yard.

Paul was educated at Kings College, Taunton. "I left a very good school without many qualifications!" he recalls.

"I had always hunted and when I left school was keen to work with racehorses. However when you're my size it's difficult to get into racing, I was quite big, just over six foot three inches, too big to ride and unless you rode you weren't much use to a racing yard. My family had no particular racing connection and that was also a hindrance when it came to getting a job with a trainer. So I thought I'd try working towards becoming a stud manager. Basically though, you would be right by saying I was in the fog about a career."

Resigned to studwork Paul went to work for Cheveley Park, Newmarket. "After being in the stud business for a short while I thought it looked more fun the other side of the fence in racing so I swapped my allegiance."

After spells with Richmond Sturdy, Les Kennard and George Todd he found a backer to set him up at Hill House Stables in Lambourn.

"Richmond Sturdy was the only chap who would have me to start with, and after a spell with Les Kennard whom I was with for a year, and George Todd, I kept going back to Richmond Sturdy at Shrewton.

"George Todd at Manton was a tremendous stableman besides being a brilliant trainer. I can never imagine why he picked me. He had advertised the post and had had at least a hundred replies.

"Little things make perfection and perfection is no little thing, that was George Todd. He worked you very hard, so much so that I think it was his aim to try and get you to leave. I used to start at 5.30 am and not get done until 11 pm some nights after I had been made to put the apprentices to bed. Then I used to get down to the pub with Jonny Haine and Jeff King." Paul stayed for a year and a half.

"I rode out four times a day, did all the normal assistant's jobs, and was worked to the point of exhaustion. He would sometimes make me lunge a yearling for two and a half hours. When he went off to the races I would hide behind a tree reading the *Sporting Life* while I let the horse have a pick of grass.

"I helped break Roan Rocket in," he recalls of his time at

47

Manton. "A brilliant miler he went on to win the St James's Palace Stakes and Sussex Stakes. Sodium was also there at the same time, he won the St Leger and Irish Derby."

The excessive attention to detail at Manton – "We even had to wash our hands before feeding" – appeared to Todd's assistant to belong to an earlier century. However frustrating as this fastidiousness was at the time, he has no doubts these days that his time spent at Manton was invaluable and that it all fitted into the jigsaw that is training. "You cannot buy experience like that," he says.

"Richmond Sturdy's was good fun, I was headlad-cum-assistant, a combination of both and virtually running the show. That too was good experience for when I set up on my own. Les Kennard, he was a good trainer, not easy to work for mind you, but he got a lot of good results from very moderate horses. You could learn a great deal about placing horses from him.

"However George Todd was the biggest influence on my career, he had the best horses. You would be pushed to find many better trainers.

"He could make horses go far beyond their natural capabilities by teaching them to relax. He would keep them out at exercise for hours. In the end the result was that he made racehorses out of selling platers even if it took years. It was typical for him to buy one out of a seller then win the Royal Hunt Cup with it the next year. These days it is not so economically possible to train to such high standards."

Manton was a great gambling yard, so much so that even the lads in those days used to stake up to £700 on fancied horses.

However although Paul was clearly influenced by the Master of Manton he is a firm believer that a young trainer should not model himself on one person alone. "It is important to pay attention to other peoples' methods but in the end it must be individual," he comments.

Hill House, which he bought from Sandy Carlos-Clark in 1968, is presently occupied by John Hills, son of Barry Hills. The trainer's white house is situated just off Folly Road on the way up to Neardown Gallops.

"A businessman, a connection of my father's, arranged my mortgage which I had to pay off out of my profits," remembers Paul. "I eventually bought him out and away we went."

He started off with three horses at Hill House, all of whom were sired by Barbary Pirate who had been in training with Sturdy and had won 11 races. "The Jockey Club wouldn't give me a licence at first but I was going to get one off them if it meant sitting outside their offices for a week," he says of the trip to London. "When I got to Portman Square my name was already on the list for not being allowed a licence. I was determined that they would give me one though and they did eventually." At the relatively tender age of 27 he was one of the youngest trainers in the country.

He saddled his first winner at Beverley in the following season, 1969, with Optimistic Pirate. "It took five years to get a string of any consequence (30 horses) together although we had five winners that year."

Paul Cole is ambitious, the flame of that ambition is hidden to some extent by his often misunderstood shyness. "There has been nothing particularly dramatic about my career," he once said, "just one long steady climb. But I am ambitious enough to want to continue climbing."

It took 22 years from the time he was granted a licence for him to win his first English Classic, the 1990 St Leger with Snurge, 23 years before he became Champion trainer for the first time in 1991, but from those humble beginnings at Hill House he has always been going forward until Classics on a regular basis and the Championship were only one short step away. When his handling of Generous helped him to the Championship in 1991, he was the first trainer outside Newmarket to enjoy the title since 1983.

Returning to those beginnings in Lambourn though. His enterprise was soon making owners sit up and take notice. He became the first trainer in Britain to install a horse-walker in 1973. He built his yard at Hill House into a 90-box complex. All the while he rarely spent more than £2,000 on any of his horses, most of which at those prices, had faults. He was one of the first trainers to enjoy success on a large scale with syndicate-owned horses and when he had horses good enough he would take them abroad where the pickings were not only richer but often easier to come by. It is no coincidence that he has won the Lord Derby Award three times for being the leading British trainer overseas.

During the Seventies his reputation was for training little winners at Beverley, Bath, Brighton, the smaller tracks. He had plenty of them and particular success with two-year-olds but it was not until the early Eighties that the winners began to flow at Grade 1 tracks like Newbury, Goodwood and Ascot. Owners were beginning to recognise what he was doing with moderate horses, what, they must have thought, would he do with some investment and better horses?

The winners flowed though and the quality improved. Nothing, they say, succeeds like success and soon he was averaging 50 winners a season. Florentine won the 1971 BBA Jubilee Handicap and Owenboliska the 1974 Zetland Gold Cup, his first 'big' races, although in 1991, they hardly rate a mention upsides the 25 Stakes races he had won. Genuine won 14 races and John de Coombe became his first Group winner. After landing the Beeswing Stakes he went on to win the Prix de la Salamandre. Crimson Beau won the Prince of Wales' Stakes and the Prix de la Cote Normande. Court Dancer was considered good enough to become his first Derby runner (Generous was his ninth) in 1974; he finished ninth.

Other horses began earning him a reputation as a skilful trainer. Shapina won the Fred Darling Stakes, Skyliner the Hungerford Stakes. Cacabina became the first of his three Wokingham Stakes winners (the other two were Queen's Pride and Bel Byou who landed a massive gamble when backed from 12–1 to 11–2 on the day of the race).

Two of his apprentices, Robert Edmondson (1972) and Dave Dinely (1976) became champions although it was Richard Quinn, whom he helped to the 1984 Apprentice Championship, that remains his principal jockey to this day.

Paul and Vanessa moved from Hill House in Lambourn to Whatcombe in time for the 1986 season. "I spent seven years trying to get out of Lambourn," he says. "It was holding me back, mid-way through my career I did mark time. I thought I was in trouble. I was lucky to get Prince Fahd at the right time to give me the ammunition to move forward."

He recalls the story of how he came to be Prince Fahd's principle trainer. "It was," he says, "a time when a lot of trainers had a lot of horses in the early Eighties. It was a boom time for racing, the Maktoums were moving in in a big way. Prince Fahd had bought a job lot of horses from America. They were a motley old bunch and I think possibly a few trainers had turned him down. Luckily a friend of Prince Khalid Abdullah, Prince Fahd's father-in-law, had put me in for the job. I went up to London for an interview and Prince Fahd didn't, at that time, think I looked quite what he expected a racehorse trainer should look like. Anyway he decided to take me on and it was one of the most exciting things to have happened to me in my racing career, to come up with an owner like that."

Paul did well with the 'ropey' bunch of horses. "From

51

PHOTOGRAPH CAPTIONS
PAGES 53–56

Page 53

Richard Quinn canters Generous down to the start past the stands at Newmarket before running in the Dewhurst Stakes on Friday 19th October, 1990, it was a nasty rainy Autumn day.

Page 54

Some 50 yards from the line in the Dewhurst and Generous starts to pull away from a hard ridden Bog Trotter (Nigel Day), Lester Piggott in the green and white colours is on Surrealist, while Willie Carson on Mujtahid is tucked in behind Generous in Sheikh Hamden Al Maktoum's colours.

Page 55

Generous now ridden by Alan Munro romps home by 5 lengths from Marju (Willie Carson) in the 1991 Epsom Derby.

Marju carries the blue and white colours associated with Sheikh Hamdan's 1989 Derby winner Nashwan.

Page 56

Prince Fahd leads in his victorious Derby colt assisted by Robert Latham who is mainly obscured.

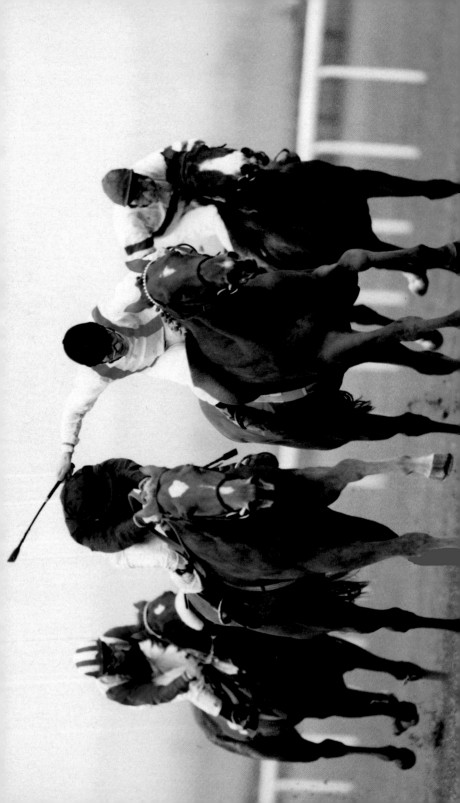

then on it has been a slow but sure progression and last year (1990) he had between about 35 and 45 horses with me – it varied. He has five trainers (Michael Bell, William Jarvis, Henry Candy and Sir Mark Prescott) of which I'm the biggest. In Anthony Penfold he has an excellent manager too."

Whatcombe had been on the market for some time. It had been bought and was for resale by Robert Sangster who had become keener on the purchase of Manton near Marlborough than he had on the somewhat smaller training centre near Great Shefford.

"My dilemma was: did I sell my yard in Lambourn while the property prices were high and then buy Whatcombe with a mortgage and sell off bits of it, houses and gallops, to enable me to get hold of it or did I take a partner in, do it up to a grade A standard and start like that? After considering the two options I chose the latter and decided I would short-cut ten years by taking on a partner in the place. That partner was Prince Fahd. We bought it in 1985, spent a year doing it up to its present standard, before we rode the whole string over from Lambourn."

Facilities at Whatcombe are among the best in the country. "Our turf," says Paul, "is the best, or equal to the best, anywhere in the country. The great thing about the place is that it is not extravagant to run. We have everything here. We have our own lake underneath the place so we have our own uncontaminated water. It is totally surrounded by grass. We have four sets of gallops, and the yard was designed largely how we wanted it."

Whatcombe has re-established itself as one of the premier training establishments in the country. Situated five miles from Wantage, a couple from Great Shefford, on the Hungerford road, it can boast some of the most wonderful facilities in the country. Unlike the big training centres of Newmarket, Lambourn in the south or Malton or Middleham in the north, those facilities are for the exclusive use of horses trained there by Paul Cole.

The place is also steeped in racing history. When Generous won the 1991 Derby he was the fifth winner of the Blue Riband to be trained there.

But a long time ago, long before Drogheda won the 1898 Grand National from here, Whatcombe was a parish of its own. A thriving Saxon village was situated in the valley that is now occupied by the stable yard. Local legend has it that the site was once occupied by a monastery and that it was linked by a secret passage-way to the spooky-looking Fawley Manor about a mile up the hill.

Part of the present Whatcombe House is built on an old Norman Church, the stones of which were taken to Lambourn to be used for the building of the Chantry Chapel, when it fell into disrepair.

Substantial evidence to back up these legends and local folklore came to light in 1935 when the then incumbent of Whatcombe, Dick Dawson, sent his lads to dig a grave for Blandford, one of the most successful and influential stallions of his time. He had sired four Derby winners (Trigo, Bleinheim, Windsor Lad and Bahram). While digging they came across the remains of human graves, subsequently dated back to the Black Death. The site is now designated an Ancient Monument.

Until Dick Dawson, of Irish ancestry, arrived in 1897, a year before he won the National, Whatcombe had been insignificant as a racing yard. Looking more like an old fashioned schoolmaster than a trainer, he was to put the place on the map as one of the country's finest training establishments. Much of Whatcombe's rich history is owed to this man. He was devoted to the place.

Soon after Drogheda had won that most prized of jump races, Dawson switched his allegiance to flat racing. It was for the Earl of Carnarvon (grandfather of the present Earl) that he won the Royal Hunt Cup at Royal Ascot with

The Solicitor and the Stewards Cup at Goodwood with Mauvezin.

During World War I he moved to Newmarket from where he saddled Fifinella to win the Derby and Oaks. Both races were run, due to the war, at Newmarket. However, in 1919 he returned to Whatcombe and within a year had won the Ascot Gold Cup with Tangiers. The following year, after George Lambton refused the offer, he was appointed trainer to the Aga Khan who had decided the time was right to realise his dream of becoming a big owner in Britain. For ten years Whatcombe witnessed one of its most productive periods. It was certainly one of the most successful owner-trainer partnerships of that era.

Among Dawson's first winners for the Aga Khan was Cos who won the Queen Mary Stakes at Ascot. She became one of the foundation mares for the Aga's bloodstock empire. Diophon won the 2,000 Guineas, Salmon-Trout the St Leger.

Mumtaz Mahal was a filly of blistering speed. When she won the Queen Mary by 10 lengths it was assumed there had been a false start. A big grey filly, she was like Desert Orchid, instantly recognisable and caught the public's imagination in a big way. When she retired to stud she did not produce any world beaters herself but she became a great dam of broodmares. Mahmoud, Migor, Petite Etoile, Nasrullah, Sir Ivor and Roberto can all be traced back to Mumtaz Mahal.

Dawson won the Oaks again in 1923 with the Vicomte de Fontarce's Brownhylda before, in 1929, he won his first Epsom Derby with Trigo, a homebred owned by a Belfast grain importer called Mr William Barnett, who went on to win the St Leger. A year later he won the race for his principal patron when Blenheim, under Harry Wragg, beat Iliad by a length.

Two years later the Aga Khan and Dawson fell out following a serious disagreement. He took away all his horses leaving Dawson to train there, the golden years behind him, on a smaller scale until he retired in 1945.

He was succeeded as master of Whatcombe by Arthur Budgett in 1951. Budgett saddled Blakeney and Morston to win the 1969 and 1973 Derbys respectively. The two horses were half-brothers and in winning the race twice with them he became only the second man to breed, own and train two Derby winners. He had other notable horses through Whatcombe including Huntercombe and his sire Derring Do. In 1969, Blakeney's year, and 22 years before the yard was to boast its next leading trainer, he won the Trainers' Championship. He retired in 1975 and handed over his string to his former assistant James Bethell, who in 1977 moved to Whitsbury and then to Chilton, near Didcot where he still trains.

You approach Whatcombe up a straight half-mile tarmac drive. At the entrance there are a cluster of lads' cottages. To the left is a cinder track along which the horses walk at exercise. There's a sleeping policeman to slow traffic down and the main house, looking something like an old rectory, and office are to the right. Continue straight on and you enter the main yard under an arch. It is a traditional square yard with a feedhouse/tackroom in the centre. It is both attractive and functional. Beyond the main yard are the muckheap, the indoor school, horsewalker, swimming pool and machinery/horsebox sheds. Cages where horses can be turned out dot the grass banks above the yard. A few wooden stables line the track to Summerdown Gallop which exits through the back of the yard.

The daily routine begins soon after 5.30 am when headlad Colin Ratcliffe, who has been with Paul Cole for 20 years, arrives to give the horses their breakfasts which consists of a bowl of oats. He is helped by two apprentices who are expected to do this extra work in return, eventually, for the opportunity to race-ride. By 6.30 am all the lads have arrived to muck out their 'first lot' which pulls out of the yard at 7.00 am during the season. On work mornings, Wednesdays and Saturdays, most horses will go to either Woolley Down or Summerdown grass gallops. On routine days they are more likely to do one, two or three good canters up the six furlong all-weather or dirt gallops close to the yard. The exceptions are Thursdays, an easy day when they may just go for a 45 minute walk, and Sundays when they stay in.

Second lot pulls out at 9.30, soon after the lads have returned from breakfast which consists of a fry-up in the canteen. There will be between 35 and 40 horses out first lot, the same second lot and about 20 third lot. After all the horses have been exercised the yards are swept and tidied up while Colin prepares lunch for the horses. Each horse will have his own individual menu, depending on his or her size, the amount of work they are doing and age. When feeding is completed at about 12.30 pm the lads return to their homes or the hostel until evening stables begin at 4.00 pm. Most lads will look after between three and four horses and will spend from 4.00 until 5.30 pm mucking them out and brushing them over. At this point the trainer, his assistant Rupert Arnold and headlad Colin will look round, checking that each horse has been properly dressed over and that it is in good health. Temperatures may be taken of horses under the weather, injured legs and wounds will be dressed and in a yard of this size, a vet will never be too far away for the more serious ailments.

After each horse has been checked, Colin gives each lad an evening feed for his own horses. When this is completed they are checked once more and then the yard is locked up for the night until Colin arrives at 5.30 am the following morning.

There are variations of course. If a horse is running abroad he may leave before dawn in order to catch the ferry or a flight. There may be activity in the yard before light, lorry engines ticking over, loading ramps banging down on the ground and the clip-clop of horse's feet on tarmac awakening horses before their regular alarm call of Colin's feed bowl bashing the side of the feed bin.

This then is the world of Whatcombe. For two years this was the home of Generous.

A SAUDI PRINCE

Prince Fahd Bin Salman Al Saud of Saudi Arabia had been owning horses in Britain for nearly a decade before Generous realised every owner's dream for him by winning the Derby. His first winner was in 1982. By 1984 Prince Fahd, a 'lucky' owner by anyone's standards, had recorded his first Pattern success when Reach, the first of many useful horses, won the Royal Lodge Stakes at Ascot. The progression upwards has continued to be equally rapid. In 1987 he won his first Classic when Zaizoom won the Derby Italiano. Three years later in 1990 he had Classic success somewhat closer to home when Knight's Baroness, a homebred, won the Irish Oaks and Ibn Bey won the Irish St Leger. Then came Generous.

But what of the man? Prince Fahd is Vice Governor ("Thank God, not entirely in charge, I share the burden") of the Eastern Province of Saudi Arabia. The position principally resolves around the security and the development of the region.

He is a good sportsman himself. He used to play football, his golf is improving he says, while he also swims and jogs regularly. He is no stranger to a horse's back either having ridden since childhood. He even rode as an amateur jockey while he was at school.

"I remember one of the big events at high school was a race we had," he recalls. "The whole race was controversial because it was so close between me, the winner, and the second but everyone had doubts about the outcome. I can even remember my colours, black and white checks. The race was run at the official track in Riyadh and in those days there were no photo finishes. Luckily we had filmed it using a 16 mm camera. To prove I had won I had to freeze the film at the winning post. I had won by a neck. Unfortunately I have lost the film now but it was a big day for me, riding a winner."

At the races he is immaculately dressed. If there was an award for the best dressed racegoer he would certainly be among the nominations. He is well educated, eloquent and, despite his background, very humble and he succeeds at maintaining a low profile on his visits to England.

He has been described as an intensely private man. On the racecourse he is known simply as Mr Fahd Salman and the biggest disappointment of not being present at Ascot for the King George was, he says, missing out on meeting the Queen afterwards.

He is also deeply religious. Following the Derby he praised Allah before thanking everyone from Paul Cole to the blacksmith for the great win. He is also a very kind man. In 1985 he donated £150,000, the value of all his winnings, to charity.

His uncle is H.M. King Fahd of Saudi Arabia, head of the ruling Abdul-Aziz family, his father-in-law is Khalid Abdullah who won the 1990 Derby with Quest For Fame and his brother Ahmed has owned some notable horses including Lear Fan and Deputy Governor.

"I first developed an interest for horses and racing as a young boy in Saudi Arabia. My first horses as an owner were in America, particularly in California, as I studied for my final year in the United States. Then, of course, I started owning horses in England."

The reasons for shifting his racing interests to Britain, and not to stay and expand in the United States where the prize-money was greater, were twofold: "Firstly, being based in Saudia Arabia, England is much closer to home," he says. "Secondly I enjoy British racing more than anything else. It is totally different to anywhere else. I

64

never really gave France a second thought because of the language barrier."

Prince Fahd has no racing interests in Saudia Arabia nowadays. "Once upon a time I did," he says, "but none now. It finished when I was sent to America to be a student of business management."

"Not even camels which, we are led to believe, the Maktoums' enjoy racing?" I asked. "There is camel racing but I don't get involved in it," he says before pointing out, "Not all Australians go kangaroo racing! The Maktoums are friends though, I have known them for years. They are neighbours, in terms of our countries, and they are brothers in the traditional Arabian way."

He runs his racing operation on tight lines. His purchases have tended not to be from the very top end of the market, although, as he has discovered, it has not precluded a high degree of success. "It is very difficult to break even in this business. You have to establish yourself more or less like a farm. Nothing happens overnight, it takes a bit of time. Of course with the pressure of the market everywhere during 1991 it makes it even harder. With Generous it would have been the most brilliant year financially for my racing business had it happened a few years ago in the mid-Eighties. Nevertheless we planted many seeds during the year and we are hoping we will capitalise on what we have done even though my budget is small compared to some of the leading owners. At one stage horses were changing hands for the same amount that I would spend on my whole budget."

Prince Fahd keeps in regular contact with British racing. He gets the racing papers, usually a day late, has articles faxed from his racing manager Anthony Penfold, and listens to his horses running on the telephone. He also watches the big races live on television – he watched a live broadcast of the King George – and is sent videos of SIS coverage.

65

It is rarely easy for Prince Fahd to get away from home to see his horses run. "Sometimes my plans work out, sometimes they don't but it is terribly difficult to get away for a particular meeting. I try hard to take the month of June off because many of the good races are run during that month. I enjoy watching the video tapes when they come from England, and I always look forward to getting them. And I will quite often sit down and watch races that I have no runners in."

When Generous won the 1990 Dewhurst Stakes it was at the very unstable time due to the Kuwait invasion by Iraq. "When I first went into racehorse ownership the Dewhurst was a race I dreamed of winning. I often used to be at the sales in Newmarket at about the time the race was run. Year after year I saw the race and always wanted a horse good enough to run in it. Of course the year I did have a runner, Generous, I felt I had to stay in Saudi Arabia and be part of whatever was going to happen. At the same time I had an appointment with my eye doctor in America. My father said I must go to my eye specialist. It would have been a good excuse to see the Dewhurst on the way but I did not feel it was right with things as they were. Instead I went to California after the United Nations had set a deadline for Iraq but it did not coincide with any racing! We had the tape of the race sent over and I took it with me to Riyadh to my mother and father. We spent a lot of the evening watching it before switching back to CNN for their news service which we were watching all the time then."

His father takes a keen interest in his son's hobby. "He is too busy to take a daily interest but whenever we have a big winner he will look at the video. He actually didn't believe a horse of mine had won the Derby."

Success at Epsom made big headlines in Saudi Arabian newspapers. "When I got home after the Derby everyone was congratulating me and I was surprised that many

66

people, many of whom knew little about racing at home or otherwise, were so interested. It was very thrilling. I wanted to duck the issue but it was so obvious that everyone was overwhelmed by it."

His racing ambition is now to breed the winner of the Derby. "It would be marvellous, we have managed to breed an Oaks winner. When Knight's Baroness won the Irish Oaks it was one of the most memorable, wonderful moments in my racing career. It did not quite compare with winning the Derby, there is something in winning the Epsom Derby which is lacking in every other race."

Prince Fahd keeps the majority of his horses with Paul Cole but he also has about 20 horses divided between Michael Bell, William Jarvis and Sir Mark Prescott in Newmarket and Henry Candy at Kingston Warren. "It would be a wonderful idea to keep all my horses at Whatcombe but then you are running a risk by keeping them all in one spot if something is wrong with stable. Having said that I have not spread them as much apart as I ought, but I believe in the yard and I believe in Paul. Therefore most are at Whatcombe."

He describes himself as an owner who likes to get involved without interfering. "I have a view though and, at the time, I thought Generous should have run before the Guineas but I understand the trainer must have the final say."

The decision to retain Alan Munro was his own. "It was entirely my own choice and happened quite quickly. He faxes me his views about horses he has ridden and we keep in touch. I don't have a hotline to Alan, I think they went out when Russia and America became friends!

"I remember I rang him on the eve of the Derby because he had been banned for a few days following an incident on Magic Ring at Goodwood. I rang to tell him to treat the Derby as just another race. 'It just happens to be at Epsom and called the Derby but don't worry about it,' I said. I didn't want him to feel any pressure from me. 'I'll tell you one thing,' he said, 'I think we are going to win it.' He had a lot of confidence. Richard Quinn is still a big part of the team though and his win on Nisnas in the Great Voltigeur is still one of my most memorable races."

As a spectating owner he gets edgy and excited. "I get a bit nervous when I go racing even when it is the smallest meeting you can think of. It is always the case and when I'm at the races I always ask myself why I have horses, I'm meant to enjoy it! But I can't help it, it is part of it all. If we win I enjoy every single minute of it, if we don't happen to win, we go back to the drawing board."

Prince Fahd's involvement with racing does not end with racehorse ownership. In 1991 he sponsored the Geoffrey Freer Stakes at Newbury and named the race after Ibn Bey. At Newmarket the Newgate Stud, the title his breeding interests are run under although he has no private stud farm as such, sponsored the Middle Park Stakes. Prince Fahd's racing manager is, as already mentioned, Anthony Penfold. It was he, along with trainer Paul Cole, who bought Generous on Prince Fahd's behalf, and as such, is a major player in the Generous story.

Much like David Nagle or Paul Cole for that matter, Anthony was not, as you might have expected, from a family steeped in racing background. Far from it in fact.

The Penfolds were originally agricultural engineers from Arundel in Sussex. His grandfather, successful in this business, was the first man in Sussex to own a car. His father and uncles however turned the attentions of the family firm to sand and gravel extraction between Chichester and Arundel. This they subsequently developed a stage further into the ready-mix concrete business.

Apart from living half way between Goodwood Race-course and the small National Hunt track of Fontwell Park, Anthony's education at the minor public school of Seaford College, had a small influence on his career, for the school was situated in the same park as the Lavington Stud.

Sometimes before his arrival at Seaford, Anthony had been taken to Fontwell for a day's racing. "It fascinated me," he recalls. "Without question it was the most exciting thing I had ever seen." The seed had been sown.

The careers officer at Seaford College was informed of young Penfold's desire to enter racing through the press-room door, his ambition to become the next Peter O'Sullevan. Aged 43 when Generous won the Derby, he now, like John Major, cannot, possibly does not wish to, recall how many qualifications he came out of college with.

"It is not easy getting into racing if you're from a non-racing background like myself," he points out. "As a result I spent a year working for my step-father's local estate agency business."

It was not the most enjoyable job he has ever had and, bored one morning in the office, he was flicking through *The Sporting Life* when he spotted an advert for the post of junior reporter on a weekly racing journal called *The Weekend Racing Blue*, so named because it was printed on blue paper. Earning the handsome sum of £17 per week, he and colleague Terry Breeze had soon helped *The Blue*'s proprietor, Tim Boydall, launch *The Pacemaker*. A forerunner of today's *Pacemaker Update*, its main asset was its glossy cover. The inner pages were still black and white newsprint.

After a couple of years he discovered that racing journalism, underneath its own glossy cover, was not exactly as he thought it would be. It was, like those early editions of *Pacemaker*, black and white newsprint on the inside.

"At this stage, aged 20," he recalls, "I was getting frustrated. I wanted to do some of the doing instead of writing about it all the time. I wanted to become a bloodstock agent."

At the same time the Jockey Club were introducing new

rules on syndication to allow multiple ownership of race-horses. He saw an opening to offer a syndicate management service. On the strength of his 'good idea' he borrowed £1,000 from the bank and headed off to see local trainers Guy Harwood at Pulborough and Alan Oughton at Findon. While Harwood did not seem keen on the idea, Alan, the late father of Hong Kong trainer David, accepted the first Penfold purchase, a syndicate owned hurdler called Glen Royal. He never won but was placed and for a while business flourished on a small scale, minor winners with other minor horses and plenty of fun. After a couple of years the inevitable happened though and a few 'sharks' had moved into the syndicate management market. In a short space of time syndicate management had earned itself a bad name. It was time to get out.

Anthony does not immediately strike you as a pushy type, possibly he has mellowed over the years but push he had to and push he did. He wrote to all bloodstock agents in England and Ireland giving self-appointed interviews. "I'll be with you on . . . at . . . unless I hear different." The fact that few bothered to reply, not because they wanted to interview him but because they had binned the letter, failed to dent his confidence. He would turn up on the doorstep at the appointed time usually much to the surprise of his intended interviewer.

At the offices of the now-defunct Anglo-Irish Bloodstock Agency in Bond Street he hung around for two hours before he could be seen. "I think just to get rid of me they said Mr Hilliard would see me. Two or three days later they rang up and said I could have another interview, this time with the chairman, and I got the job."

It was the sort of job that provided a wonderfully broad grounding in all departments of the bloodstock agent's business. Owen Helman, who now lives in Guernsey, was a specialist in pedigree and taught the rookie agent about bloodlines. Frank More O'Ferrall was a larger than life figure. He lived life to the full, had great presence and was a gifted raconteur, it went without saying that he could get a good deal whether buying or selling horses. The Anglo-Irish, at this time during the Sixties, was dealing with some wealthy American clients, among them Bing Crosby.

Anthony remained based at Bond Street for five years where he learned a great amount. However he could not see a future in a firm that was reluctant to give its own youngstock enough responsibility.

At the same time a friend from Sussex, John Woodman, son of the late trainer Syd Woodman, suffered a career ending fall at Worcester. A promising jump jockey at the time he was suddenly forced, aged 25, to seek an alternative career. The pair, great friends since childhood, went into partnership. With £2,000 each they formed the Goodwood Bloodstock Agency.

They spent nine years in partnership. For much of their business they returned to syndicate management following new changes in the rules made by the Jockey Club. For the original £4,000 they bought four yearlings which went into training with John's father Syd. They included Belle Bretonne who won five races and was second in the Newbury Autumn Cup, won over £11,000 in prize-money and was sold for 21,000 gns at the end of it. Others included Gallico, bought for 1,000 gns. He turned his feet out like Charlie Chaplin but won three years successively at the Newmarket July Meeting. Another was Passing Shot. Although she only won a seller on the flat at Goodwood she went on to become a top juvenile hurdler by beating Rasti in the Stroud Green Hurdle at Newbury and by finishing in front of Night Nurse in the Triumph Hurdle.

By this stage Anthony was straying further afield. He was beginning to make trips to the yearling sales in Kentucky but syndicates were again getting an unfavourable press and the Goodwood Bloodstock Agency began to specialise in limited partnership ownership.

One of his first American purchases was Sir Samuel, bought from Fasig-Tipton in 1979. Sir Samuel won at Newmarket on Guineas day, finished second in the Chesham Stakes at Royal Ascot and wound up a pretty useful two-year-old. The following year orders, which Anthony had justification in thinking might start flooding in, failed to appear. Off their own bat Goodwood Bloodstock decided to put up their own cash to pinhook a filly. It was a gamble but it paid off. She cost $16,000 and they managed to resell her for 30,000 gns. Named Full of Reason she was bought by Newmarket trainer Luca Cumani and went on to become Group placed as a three-year-old. "The profit from that one deal kept John and I in business for a year!" recalls Anthony.

"I was wanting to concentrate more on the agency side of things though, while John was keener on supporting his father's operation. Profits increased every year but in the end we had different aims and split up. We had had a lot of fun though, we learned a lot the hard way with our own money which also taught us to be very careful. All the time you knew that one mistake and the chances were that you'd go under."

The next four years saw Anthony trading under his own name but doing much of the same work, buying for resale, in America, Australia, playing the markets. It was following the 1983 season that his career took another turn although at the time it was neither expected nor particularly sought. He was quite happy doing his own thing, making a name for himself, his own boss, when out of the blue he received a phone call from Grant Pritchard-Gordon, racing manager for Khalid Abdullah who was already in the process of building up a large bloodstock empire. Would Anthony like an interview with Prince Fahd Salman, Abdullah's son-in-law? Prince Fahd had a few horses with

Paul Cole, was keen to expand and was looking for a racing manager just to guide things along a little. "But I'm not looking for a job," said Anthony more than content with what he was already doing. "Well," said Grant, "I think you at least ought to come for the interview – it won't be any ordinary job."

Anthony had not envisaged working for anyone other than himself again but, at the same time, common sense told him he had nothing to lose by going to the interview. Within five minutes of meeting Prince Fahd it was clear prospective employer and employee had hit it off.

"If I was going to work for someone else again it was clear it had to be for someone I respected and knew I could get along with," he remembers thinking at the time.

There were 'I's to dot and 'T's to cross. Anthony was offered the job on a trial basis for a year on the condition that he could keep his principal clients which included representing Mill Ridge Stud in Europe, a retainer for Paul de Moussac and a certain amount of work for Gerald Leigh. If he got the job after a year he would, for his part of the bargain, cease to work for these clients.

So in February 1984, shortly before the start of a new flat season, the name Penfold was added to the equation that already included Prince Fahd and Paul Cole. The new racing manager's brief was twofold: firstly Prince Fahd's ambition was to win the Epsom Derby, secondly he wanted to try and make the operation break-even.

INTO TRAINING

The purchase of Generous at Goffs Cartier Million Sales was like any other Cole–Penfold operation on behalf of Prince Fahd.

"We inspect them together," says Paul. "He leans towards some, I lean towards others. If I don't like one or if Anthony doesn't like one, we don't buy it, it is as simple as that. It is a collective effort. All the good horses except Reach and Sarab which I bought before Anthony became Prince Fahd's manager, have been bought like that.

"With the occasional obvious exception we are looking for the sort of yearling that will stay a mile and half as a three-year-old," says Anthony before poking fun at himself. "We might end up salvaging a two mile handicapper out of it at the end of the day!

"It is a numbers game. To have any chance of breaking even" (he refers to one of Prince Fahd's two aims) "you have got to have a top horse every year. Now, the way the market has gone recently, even that is not enough."

There is no doubting that as a team at the sales Paul and Anthony are successful. They clearly think along similar lines and, equally clearly, their relationship is as good as any trainer–racing manager in the country whether it be in the unsaddling enclosure or on the tennis court. They both have a good eye for a horse.

Their record speaks for itself. In 1984 they bought amongst others, Nomination, Nomrood and Nisnas, in 1985 Bint Pasha, Ibn Bey, the first English trained colt to win £1 million, Broken Hearted and Beechi, horses that will go down as some of the greats to be trained at

Whatcombe. The following year they bought the yearling Insan for $42,000.

In 1987, they did have a bit of a hiccup but haven't we all? A disastrous year for purchasing decent horses was reflected in a poor year with three-year-olds in 1989. "There was," recalls Anthony with total honesty, "not a soldier among them! Not a glimmer of hope."

In 1988 they got back on the winning trail with the purchase of Zoman, in 1989 they bought Generous which we shall deal with shortly and in 1990 they bought Dilum whose success was backed up by some useful home-breds beginning to come through in Magic Ring and Fair Cop.

The breeding operation is still small-scale compared to that of Sheikh Mohammed and Sheikh Hamdan. Although it has seen a certain amount of investment from Prince Fahd recently in broodmares he owns no stud. There are 40 mares split between the Sandley Stud at Gilingham, Dorset and Mill Ridge in Kentucky, America. Knight's Baroness, winner of the Irish Oaks, was from Prince Fahd's first crop of homebreds. "I was more emotionally moved by her success in the Irish Oaks than I was by Generous' win in the Derby," recalls Anthony before adding: "We were quoted various prices for Doff The Derby before the 1991 season. At that stage, although obviously a good broodmare, she had only bred a Dewhurst winner and not a Derby winner. At the price she was out of our league. Paying £2 million for a mare would have been out of proportion to our operation, it is not the Prince's style to pay £1 million for any horse.

"However he feels uncomfortable with high priced yearlings although with broodmares you are looking at more of an investment."

Generous was selling on a Wednesday at Goffs Cartier Million Sales, 11 October 1989. Anthony and Paul arrived at Kill the previous Sunday, three days before. Anthony has an office at Goffs from where he is able to keep in constant touch with Prince Fahd.

"At first we were prepared to go to Ir 200,000 gns, then we thought Ir 150,000 gns would be our maximum for him. But we liked the colt, he was one of the best in the sale, so we upped it again. I think we eventually said we would be happy with Ir 250,000 gns but, if desperate, Ir300,000 gns would be the absolute maximum. We changed the limits a good three times." The figures are crossed out and re-scribbled across the page of his catalogue.

Anthony is in contact with Prince Fahd through the day, sometimes three or four times an hour, sometimes he does not speak to him for four hours. "We discuss budgets and figures," says Anthony, "although we have occasionally bought something that we have not discussed. He has a copy of the catalogue with him and sometimes he likes to be on the end of the phone when a horse is being sold."

The other notes pencilled in Anthony's catalogue under the Caerleon colt read: "Quality, scope, great outlook, lovely mover, tiny splints."

"One remembers his presence more than anything else and you were first of all hit by his colour. I think in the end it was his colour that enabled us to be able to buy him. I don't think people thought his colour was particularly manly for a colt.

"But he had a bold outlook. You see some colts whose attitude puts you off. He handled himself well and was not affected by the stress that a sale sometimes puts on a yearling. If they can handle that well the chances are that they will handle training well. He was a loose mover and a great walker. Although I wrote 'scopey' down it is amazing how little he has changed, even at the end of his three-year-old career he was still looking more like a precocious two-year-old. He wasn't a lean Slip Anchor type."

On the day of the sale as lot 441 approached Hamish

Alexander was getting jumpy. "Some of our best horses we have bought have been from pinhookers, Broken Hearted for example," says Anthony. "It does not bother me that their profit is there for everyone to see, it certainly doesn't influence my decision as to how much we'll pay for a yearling. I think they are brave people, Hamish and Timmy Hyde seem to have the job sussed between them, if that is possible."

Generous was knocked down to a Penfold bid for their original guess, Ir 200,000 gns. He was one of eight bought at that sale by the pair. One, an expensive Law Society colt named Gold Law won his maiden and looked potentially useful until he broke a leg at the start of the 1991 season. Of the remaining six none 'made it'. "But for Generous we wouldn't have been too proud of the effort!" says Anthony with the benefit of hindsight.

Prince Fahd's luck really was in Generous' colour. If he had been a strong bay the chances were that the Maktoums would have snapped him up, as they did most other including Marju who was to run second to Generous in the Derby. "Everything else about the horse was right," says Anthony. "I can only assume they passed him by because of his colour."

At the time both racing manager and trainer were delighted with their purchase. "But in November when we had finished buying we could not say categorically that we had a champion in Generous. We had other horses we liked as much, and although he was our second most expensive (the Law Society cost Ir 300,000 gns)."

In the meantime, Generous, now the property of Prince Fahd, spent a week at the Tara Stud in Ireland before returning to England and to Whatcombe where he was to spend his next two years. When a yearling arrives at Whatcombe in October or early November he would be mistaken if he thought he was leaving the madhouse of the sales-ring for the tranquillity of training. Whatcombe at this time of year is a hive of activity, it is perhaps their busiest period. Horses are still running at home and abroad, some lads are away taking their charges to the horse-in-training sales, others, unable to get away for a holiday during high summer, are on leave. Manpower is at a premium and it may be a day or two after his arrival that a colt finally get to be lunged. However after the sales a few days in the box does not harm.

A colt confined to his box for a day or two awaiting his breaking will be fed a mash every evening by Colin Ratcliffe. It consists of boiled linseed and barley, bran, crushed oats, vegetable oil, and a few other goodies like molasses. The older horses, out of training while they enjoy a short break, will be fed a mash three times a week anyway, the yearlings every evening. During the day they will get hay and water but, while they are doing so little, they will get no breakfast or lunch.

When Generous arrived he had already been well tutored by Hamish, breaking-in was a mere formality. Dominic ffrench-Davis, a pupil assistant now at Whitsbury with David Elsworth, was responsible for breaking him in.

"He was," remembers Dominic, "a smashing, well handled colt. He was a big yearling with plenty of bone. He didn't grow much afterwards, he just filled out. He did not stick out as being very tricky."

After being lunged for a couple of days the next stage was to put a roller on Generous. This is a soft padded broad strap which is tied around a horse's girth to accustom him to having a saddle applied at the next stage. After he had been driven with a saddle and side-reins, an assessment made of his mouth and behaviour, Tony Bradley, one of Whatcombe's travelling headlads, lay across him in his box. As his confidence grew Tony was then able to sit on him properly in the stable. This he would have done for a couple of days to give Generous time to familiarise himself with the weight on his back.

Within a week to 10 days Generous would have been broken in and ridden away.

"One in 15 might be tricky," says Kevin McAuliffe, the present pupil-assistant at Whatcombe. "Horses like Generous coming from the experienced handlers at the sales are half-broken anyway. It is usually the homebreds that are difficult."

The minute Generous was ridden away he was put on to lunch, maybe a handful of beat-pulp and half a bowl of oats, by Colin who gradually weans them on to a proper diet as they begin to do more work.

The older horses, two-year-olds and three-year-olds, as Generous was to be the following autumn, are turned out for their holidays. Geldings and fillies go into paddocks at Whatcombe and the colts into the cage pens. The bulk of first lot will be yearlings although a dozen older horses are kept on the go for all-weather racing.

The first day he would have been led by a hack quietly up the all-weather. When the string of yearlings has swelled and more have been broken-in, they begin going up the all-weather twice, trotting initially, then hack-cantering the second time up. They walk through simulated stalls on the way back down.

As they grow and get stronger they work quicker until after Christmas they start going upsides each other. The slower, more backward types will find themselves dropping out the back and they will be allowed to come on in their own time. Generous, however, as one of the more precocious two-year-olds of his generation, would have been picked out by the trainer on his return from a three-week January holiday.

By the end March, early April he would have been doing steady work on the grass. All the while Paul would have been looking for the tell-tale signs that signify he is pushing a two-year-old too fast.

"In the spring I travelled to Whatcombe several times to

79

see how they were all progressing," says Anthony. "We discussed Generous several times because we thought he should be trained like a mile and half three-year-old not as a precocious two-year-old. He had speed though and was doing it all so easily we thought we might as well carry on."

Throughout the winter the yearlings are mucked out in lines by teams. It was not until March, just before the start of 1990 Flat season that each lad was asked to state which two-year-olds he would prefer to look after. It works on seniority, a long serving lad being more likely to get his request. If he has looked after a blood-relation of that particular two-year-old he will also be given preference.

Robert Latham says: "Basically I liked his attitude, he was very quiet and looked strong so I asked if I could look after him. He was so easy going and has always been superb to look after from day one until he left in November 1991." And the name? Generous. "Prince Fahd names most of them, I have very little to do with it," says Anthony. "He sometimes gives them easy to pronounce Arabic names, otherwise they are English. Quite frankly I was surprised we got Generous."

People read a lot into a horse's name. Some people will tell you that had Desert Orchid been called Grey Drizzle or something less inspiring he would not have been half the horse. Badly named horses are rarely champions. Hamish Alexander remembers: "When I saw that he had been called Generous I thought to myself that's either a champion racehorse or the waste of a very good name!"

THREE WINS IN 1990

"When a two-year-old comes in the yard their pedigree is only a guide. So what you do is start training them and as they progress you get more and more of a picture as to the way the horse is developing, what he is and what he isn't. Now backward horses start getting sore shins, knee problems, joints and other minor irritations so you leave them alone. They are telling you they are not mature enough to be trained.

"More precocious horses keep coming forward. Now with regard to Generous, one half-sister had won in America and the other, Wedding Bouquet, had won a decent two-year-old race in Ireland. A lot of Caerleons show good speed early on so I kept training him and he kept coming forward and was showing a lot of foot. Without putting him under any pressure at all he came to himself. So we decided to run him in the Garter Stakes at Ascot on 2nd May 1990," recalls Paul Cole.

The Garter Stakes over five furlongs is a graduation race run on the same day as the White Rose Stakes which is generally regarded as a minor Derby trial. It was open to two-year-old colts who had not won more than one race at starting and carried a penalty value of £7,245 to the winner. Six horses were declared for the race including the William Jarvis' well thought of (at the time) Grey Rooster who had won a Newmarket maiden on his only previous outing. Richard Hannon also fielded Les Animaux Nuages who had won his maiden at Newbury. Of the six to line up Generous was the only one making his debut. Stable jockey Richard Quinn was in the saddle as he was on five of the six occasions Generous was to run as a two-year-old.

It was to turn out to be a fine day for owner, trainer and jockey, all returning home with three winners apiece. River Nomad kicked off by winning the Insulpak Stakes, a graduation for three-year-olds, she was followed by Generous in the Garter Stakes while Sultan's Son stormed home under Alan Simpson to win the Chobham Apprentices Stakes. Richard Quinn had also won the White Rose Stakes on Starstreak which was the middle leg of his first ever Ascot treble.

Generous started the Garter Stakes at 6–1 third favourite, relatively unfancied at a price that lived up to his name. Grey Rooster was the 5–4 favourite. For a debutant he was remarkably fast away from the stalls despite 'wobbling' somewhat greenly away from them. Nevertheless to break in the front rank in a race where he was the only one never to have been on a racecourse before demonstrated just how well he had been schooled in this department. Over the minimum trip of five furlongs and on good to firm ground he was clearly going to have to be close to the pace throughout.

After a furlong the field began to settle into some order, four lengths covered them and they were headed by South Crofty one off the rails, ridden by Alan Munro, who led Generous on his outside, by half a length. On the inside Don't Give Up, level with Generous, was showing good early speed while the favourite Grey Rooster, ridden by John Reid, was a further length away to the outside of Generous.

At the two-furlong marker Generous found himself in front in a race for the first time and it did not seem to bother him that he, the raw recruit, was having to lead. At this stage Richard Quinn began to ride him out quite forceably but without having to resort to the whip. A furlong out saw Generous change legs and gears as he began to assert this authority over the tiring South Crofty and Grey Rooster who was in the process of disappointing his fans. Les Animaux Nuages, who with Pat Eddery had been biding his time nearer the rear than the front, put in a strong late challenge but he was never going to head Generous and failed to get there by half a length. In the last hundred yards Richard had shown Generous the whip but he had not had to smack him. It was a highly satisfactory result for Generous' connections. He looked like he would be better suited by further, he had not had a hard race, he had learned something about racing which you can't teach them at home. Despite some signs of greenness which were only to be expected it was a highly promising result. He clearly had speed and the margin of his success probably belied the fact that he had won a little cleverly. It was clear he would come on for this run.

"He won well although he ran with a little inexperience but you'd expect that," recalls Richard. "The Guv'nor teaches them their job and it is never usually a problem when one hits the front for the first time. His run was full of promise especially as he was the only unraced horse in the field. He overcame that disadvantage and I was able to ride him out hands and heels without having to use my stick."

It was a remarkably early racecourse debut for a future Derby winner. Even Mill Reef, the most recent precocious Derby winner before Generous, made his first two-year-old appearance nearly a fortnight later than our hero when successful at Salisbury. "We weren't to know," recalls Paul, "that he would get a mile and a half eventually. He had shown this tremendous turn of foot and so we went to Ascot for the Coventry Stakes seven weeks later where he would be up against specialised sprinters. Mill Reef had won the race as a two-year-old."

The Coventry, on the opening day and one of the feature two-year-old races at Royal Ascot, on 19th June

1990 represented not only a step up in class for Generous but also in distance, and a change in jockey. Richard Quinn had been injured in a fall at Sandown earlier in the week in which he was concussed and broke a small bone in his hand. The consequence was that he would have to miss the next seven days and the whole of the Ascot meeting. It was another Scot though, Willie Carson, who got the job.

Favourite for the race, worth £24,368 to the winner (in 1970 Mill Reef picked up £4,991 and 14 shillings for his efforts) was Mac's Imp, trained by Bill O'Gorman in Newmarket and ridden by Alan Munro who had been contracted to ride for O'Gorman at the start of that season. O'Gorman is a specialist two-year-old trainer and has built his reputation around consistent, speedy youngsters and in Mac's Imp he had a remarkably fast individual even by his standards. At 8–1 Generous was fourth favourite.

Mac's Imp, with the benefit of four races already under his belt, was travelling better than any of his 12 rivals throughout the race. Willie had Generous prominent in the first four on the standside, a couple of lengths off Munro who was endeavouring to make all the running. Willie began pushing from half-way, still a length and a half down on Mac's Imp who had slightly increased his lead again to two lengths with a quarter of a mile to run. From here on in no horse looked likely to catch Mac's Imp. Although Generous stayed on nicely to hold Bold Nephew comfortably in third place, with 50 yards to run Willie had accepted the situation and eased Generous down. At the line the winning margin was two lengths to give Alan Munro his first Pattern success. Despite having won over five furlongs first time out it now looked likely that Generous would need further than six furlongs. Nevertheless he had shown commendable form in a Group 3 contest. What Paul Cole was to hear in the winner's enclosure was music to his ears although he had shown surprise immediately after the race that his horse had been beaten. "I could have been closer if I had moved earlier. Make no mistake," said Willie Carson as he took the saddle from Generous' back, "this is definitely a very, very good horse. He's a Group 1 horse and you're a lucky chap." Willie looked at the horse and stalked off to the weighing room.

Generous continued to please at home after Ascot. The plan was hatched to take him to Glorious Goodwood on Thursday 2nd August for the Group 3 Lanson Vintage Stakes over seven furlongs. It was, thought Cole, the ideal distance and to be honest on paper it did not look the hottest Vintage Stakes ever run. With the exception of Peter Walwyn's Mukaddamah who had run once and won once at Nottingham, the remaining four runners had all been exposed to a large degree.

Generous was second favourite in a field that included Neville Callaghan's Corrupt who was also destined to line up with Generous in the following year's Derby. Mac's Imp who had beaten Generous in the Coventry had, the previous day, won the Richmond Stakes in good style. His form was indisputably the best of the six runners but the gamble on Mukaddamah was on the promise he had shown first time out and not on solid form.

The ground at Goodwood was firmer than Generous had encountered on a racecourse before and it was a stifling hot day. Generous got very geed up in the preliminaries and was on his toes. "He was a horse with a lot of nervous energy," recalls Paul. "He got into a boiling situation, into a lather."

Generous's defeat that day will go down as one of the biggest shocks of the Whatcombe trainer's career. "I could not believe it," he says.

Reunited with Richard Quinn, Prince Fahd Salman's colt was, as he always had been, blisteringly fast away from the stalls. After the field had sorted itself out Richard

85

found himself upsides the wide outsider Andrath and Michael Roberts in front. Generous did not care to be taken on by Andrath and fought for his head; he was running too freely up the hill for his own good.

At the quarter mile marker Generous had, at last, established superiority over Andrath but in doing so he had played right into the hands of Mukaddamah ridden by Willie Carson who could not, after what he had said following the Coventry, have been over hopeful of success beforehand. Sat comfortably on the rails behind Generous, Willie made use of a convenient opening at the same time that Andrath gave best. Switching him to the outside of the pair Willie sent Mukaddamah on just below the distance and the writing was on the wall. Generous appeared to run weary in the last furlong and was passed by Flying Brave who, under John Reid, had been biding his time at the rear of the field for much of the way. Flying Brave flew at the finish but it never really looked as if he would ever catch Mukaddamah who won by a length and a half. There was a further three lengths back to Generous in third. To say this run was disappointing to his connections was an understatement.

"I put the defeat down partially to circumstance, partially to myself and partially to Richard, a collective blame if you like for that one," says Paul. "It was hot, he doesn't like flies, Richard let him run a bit too freely.

"However he had shown a tremendous amount of foot through the early stages of the race and I thought to myself, this horse has a stack of speed, we'll run him in the Prix Morny at Deauville."

The Prix Morny Agence Français is a Group 1 race run over a straight six furlongs at Deauville on the north coast of France. In 1990 it was run on Sunday 19th August and was worth £107,181 to the winner. Paris racing basically moves lock, stock and barrel to Deauville in August for what can only be described as a festival of racing, where the holiday atmosphere is combined with the seriousness of top class racing and high living. In 1991 the race went to Arazi, who went on, through the latter part of the season, to steal some of our hero's thunder.

However, despite the upset at Goodwood some seventeen days earlier, Paul still had enormous faith in Generous and felt that he could justify his presence in a field of tremendous quality. It included some of the best of British two-year-olds as well as French including the unbeaten Hector Protector trained by François Boutin.

"Unbeknown to me at the time," says Paul, "the racecourse stables were in the sales paddock. The French sell late at night and we think that the continuous noise, lights and the clearing up afterwards meant that Generous was uable to relax until about three o'clock in the morning. Anyhow the long and the short of it was that he never went a furlong in the race."

Of all his efforts the Prix Morny will go down as Generous' worst. He looked uncomfortable from the start and before they had gone a furlong it was clear that the chestnut on the stands side rails might well have stayed at home. He fretted beforehand like he had done at Goodwood and was the first to come off the bridle on the good to soft ground. He could only finish tenth of 12 behind Hector Protector and Freddie Head who dominated the race from the front-rank to beat Divine Danse one and a half lengths with Acteur Français a further length and a half back in third. It was not a great race for the English, indeed it has not been since My Swallow last won it for us under Lester Piggott in 1970. Dominion Gold fared best in sixth while Line Engaged could manage only eighth.

Richard Quinn remembers the race well. "He never went a yard, with hindsight it may be that he just was not a good traveller. He had also, I think, had a bad trip to Goodwood."

It was back to the drawingboard for Generous. "We got

87

PHOTOGRAPH CAPTIONS
PAGES 89–92

Page 89

Paul Cole who has emerged in the last two or three years as a great, rather than good trainer, which he had been for many years, poses for the camera with Generous.

Page 90

Later the same morning Generous picks grass held by his regular work rider Tommy Jennings watched by Paul Cole. The author is in the right foreground with the light blue jacket and quartered cap.

Page 91

Generous puts up perhaps his greatest performance at Ascot in the King George VI and Queen Elizabeth Diamond Stakes when winning by seven lengths from Sanglamore on 27th July, 1991. Between winning the Epsom Derby on 5th June and this race Generous had won the Irish Derby at the Curragh on 30th June.

Page 92

Her Majesty The Queen congratulates Alan Munro after his and Generous' breathtaking performance in the King George.

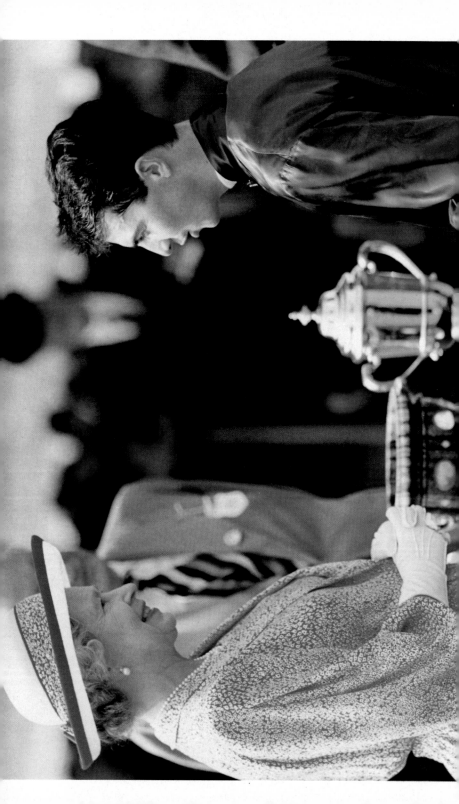

him back to England," recalls Paul, "and, taking an outside view of this, I thought we would rest him, freshen him up and retrain him. I swapped his work jockeys, put Tommy Jennings up on him and began to concentrate on the horse. I started to give the horse everything I'd got. Don't forget we didn't know at this stage that he was going to win next year's Derby. He was quite a nice two-year-old then who I was trying to get back on the right tracks."

After a brief holiday he was aimed at the Reference Point Stakes at Sandown. The race was ideal. Run on Tuesday 18th September it had given him ample time to recover from Goodwood and Deauville, it was over a mile on good ground, it was close to home and it cut up to a small field. "I said to Richard, drop him out the back and switch him off. Ride him with a lot of confidence because we are very confident."

Once again Generous was out of the stalls like lightning upsides Tapatch and Pat Eddery who was in the process of riding a four-timer. He clearly intended to make the running. Generous had jumped out a length ahead of Rahdari ridden by Walter Swinburn and the outsider Battlers Green. The fact that he had left the stalls so quickly had not helped Richard to settle the horse. However after a brief 'fight' Generous accepted the situation, dropped the bridle and settled in last place.

After a furlong five lengths separated the leader Tapatch from Generous the back-marker. The others, Rahdari and Battlers Green sat in Indian file behind Eddery and this was how they travelled to the bend.

Still in single file rounding the sharp Sandown bend as they left the railway, Battlers Green was the first to come off the bridle. In doing so he drifted off the rail leaving it clear for Generous. Off the bend and Swinburn began to move Rahdari up smoothly to join Tapatch and the pace quickened as the race developed between these two. Richard, meanwhile still bode his time a couple of lengths

93

off this pair on the inside rail having passed the struggling Battlers Green. Initially it looked like Rahdari, a newcomer, would have little trouble taking Tapatch but it was not until a furlong out that he finally overcame the early leader. It appeared that he had not done so with as much ease as his jockey thought at first he might. Richard had changed his hands on Generous two furlongs out, he was certainly riding with plenty of confidence as he had been instructed, and at the same time moved off the rail in order to have room when he so required, to let Generous go. Still he sat tucked in behind Rahdari. He eventually made his move inside the final furlong where Rahdari had taken up the running. In a few strides he had drawn level, a few strides further and he was ahead. Richard really only had to shake the reins at him. He won by a comfortable length and a half. The race had been just what the doctor had ordered for Generous, a small field had allowed him to settle, he had not had a hard race and his confidence was back. His trainer had succeeded in getting him back on the right track. His next decision was going to be an important one.

"He came off the bridle for about 50 yards, passed the horses in front of him and came back on the bridle. I was very pleased with him," Paul said.

The papers, following this smooth success, suggested that the Cartier Million for which Generous was qualified was his likely target. Up at Partridge Close Stud, Hamish Alexander was gleefully rubbing his hands together and counting the pennies Generous might earn him should he run in the Cartier Million. There was a very valuable vendor's prize which he stood to collect. Corwyn Bay and The Caretaker, both, like Generous, sons of Caerleon, had won the first two runnings of the race.

"We were very pleased with him then, we didn't put him under any work pressure at home, kept him fresh and well and headed towards the Cartier Million or the

Dewhurst," recalls his trainer. "At that particular time I was favouring the Cartier Million mainly for commercial reasons. He was 4–1 favourite. But what put me off was that it was such a micky-mouse race with regard to draw, size of field, and this, that and the other. I then thought that this horse had had enough of that sort of thing and travelling to Ireland might upset him again. So without wanting to make another mistake with him, I'd go for the Dewhurst Stakes. At least we would get a proper race and a proper idea of the horse's ability. Then we would be able to make suitable plans for next year."

Little did he know Hamish Alexander was pulling his hair out in desperation when he realised the big bonus was no longer on from his point-of-view.

The ground at Newmarket on Friday 19th October was officially good but steady rain had softened it up during the afternoon. It was, Paul thought at the time, against his horse. The Three Chimneys Dewhurst Stakes is a Group 1 race over seven furlongs. The Rowley Mile racecourse is no easy seven furlongs and the fact that Generous had won over a mile, proving he stayed, and initially over five furlongs, proving he had speed, was to be in his favour.

Nevertheless Generous was friendless in the market at 50–1. His Coventry form was 'exposed' and it was hard to tell how impressive his Sandown confidence-booster had been; he had not after all, beaten a whole lot. But Willie Carson's words: "He's a Group 1 horse" were about to come true.

The Dewhurst was worth £117,609 to the winner. Eight runners lined up for the race. Robert Armstrong's un-beaten Mujtahid was sent off the 4–5 favourite. His record going into the race made him look a worthy favourite. He had put up what was described as the most impressive two-year-old performance of the season when trouncing Mac's Imp, who had beaten Generous by two lengths in the Coventry, and by seven lengths in the July Stakes. He had defeated Vintage Only well to win the Gimcrack Stakes at York and had since had a short holiday. Henry Cecil also fielded Sedair, unbeaten in two outings, to be ridden by Steve Cauthen. Lester Piggott was now back in the swing of things after coming out of his retirement and was booked for Barry Hills's Surrealist. Lester's son-in-law, trainer William Haggas, had his best chance yet of a first Group 1 success with Bog Trotter whom he had supplemented for the contest. He had won the Laurent Perrier Champagne Stakes at Doncaster's Leger meeting, a race that was subsequently rocked by a doping scandal when the disappointing favourite, Bravefoot, was tested positive to a make-you-go-slower drug and had then been beaten over the course and distance in a false run race by Peter Davies. From Ireland Go South, who had finished fifth in the Cartier Million, was out to redeem his hitherto unbeaten record.

Mujtahid's biggest danger it was thought would come from Alex Scott's unbeaten Anjiz, also owned by the Maktoum family, although the question mark over this speedy colt was his stamina.

The plan was once again to ride Generous, the most experienced member of the eight, from off the pace as Richard had done at Sandown. After two furlongs the tightly grouped field were headed by Bog Trotter and Nigel Day. At the back Generous was on the far side of the group which was coming up the centre of the course. He was no more than six lengths off the leader. Bog Trotter was gradually increasing the pace at the front, his stamina was guaranteed. Three furlongs out Day began to ask him to go about his business and make it a real test in the by-now tacky ground. Two furlongs out, at the famous 'bushes' it must be said that it looked like he had the measure of everything. Richard had anticipated the moment Day struck for home and had steadily moved into a challenging position. A furlong out and Mujtahid was well beaten, he had been chased along by Willie Carson from three furlongs out, but it still looked like Bog Trotter's race. His lead was still two lengths. Richard went to work on Generous, peeling him off a series of galvanising back-handers with his whip. It had the desired effect and when, half a furlong out he was still a length down, he was able to put stick down and ride him hands and heels, his challenge had a relentless, unstoppable look about it. He was wearing Bog Trotter down with each stride. He finally hit the front 50 yards from the line, outstaying the gutsy Bog Trotter by an increasing three-quarters of a length at the line. Surrealist and Lester finished two and a half lengths away in third with the favourite Mujtahid a further two lengths back in fourth. The remainder finished well strung out.

"The ground was a bit soft for him and it took him a while to catch Bog Trotter," recalls Paul. "With the ground a bit faster he always shows a bit more speed. In the end he did it well and despite the win few people except me really had any faith in the horse for the following year."

Generous' victory had produced the biggest upset in the 115-year history of the Dewhurst but there was no denying it was not earned, few excuses could be found for the vanquished. The race had a reputation for being Europe's top two-year-old test. Mill Reef, Grundy and The Minstrel, all winners in the Seventies helped establish this reputation while Stormbird, Deisis and El Gran Senor were winners back in the early Eighties, the last Classic winner to have won this race first.

The signs however were good for the winter. It rounded off a wonderful second half of the season spell of success for Whatcombe. Knights Baroness had won the Irish Oaks, Ibn Bey won a Group 1 in Dusseldorf and then proceeded to take his career earnings towards the £1 million barrier in the Irish St Leger. Both belonged to Prince Fahd Salman. At home Snurge had given Paul and

Richard their first British Classic when he won the St Leger and then went on to finish a gallant third in the Arc.

Bookmakers, however, did not reflect the trainer's enthusiasm. He was offered at 50–1 by Corals and Hills for the 1991 2,000 Guineas, Ladbrokes were a little more impressed, quoting him at 33–1.

Paul Cole knew what he'd got in Generous and Robert Latham, the horse's lad, was dreaming of Classics.

"Guineas?" a damp hack asked in the winner's enclosure at Newmarket. "Yes, I suppose so," was the contented trainer's reply.

THE GUINEAS

Following his triumphant return from Newmarket and the Three Chimneys Dewhurst Stakes, Generous was let down and given a short holiday at Whatcombe. He had had a hard season, run six times starting at Ascot at the beginning of May and had not finished until late October. Remarkably he had withstood all six races without a single physical set-back or hold up. He had lost his way in between time but he finished, as he had started, by winning. Any problems he had suffered, it was generally agreed, had been mental but those appeared to be behind him now.

Bookmakers had been unimpressed with what they had seen in the Dewhurst. This was despite the fact that few excuses could be offered for the vanquished. His trainer had confirmed after the race that the 50–1 winner would probably have the 2,000 Guineas as an objective the following season. 'Probably' is as good as you will get seven months in advance of the following season's second Classic. Coral's and Hills offered him at 50–1, Ladbrokes at 33–1. Marju, John Dunlop's younger brother of Salsabil who had proved herself the outstanding three-year-old filly of 1990, was already a warm favourite at 6–1 although he had only run and won once.

Racehorses of 1990, a publication by Timeform suggested that "enterprising placement might be necessary if he's to win more races, for as a consequence of his Dewhurst win he'll now have to carry a penalty in all bar the best." It went on, in its summing up to suggest Generous might emulate Ian Balding's 1989 Dewhurst winner Dashing Blade who went on to win some prestigious prizes in France and Italy.

"Subconsciously you're thinking about your horses all the time," says Paul. "During the winter I was thinking about Generous a lot and gradually I began to think I should concentrate on the Derby with the horse rather than the Guineas. We would take that in on the way but if we had meant serious business with the Guineas, it would have meant giving him a prep-race over seven furlongs in the mud somewhere and apart from anything else we knew he didn't like that going particularly. It would have made his season that much longer too."

After his break Generous was soon back into the routine of the string, out first lot every day hacking quietly. During the spring all the signs suggested he had trained on. He continued in the same vein that he had as a two-year-old. He began working well but it was in his preparation for the 2,000 Guineas that he suffered the only physical set-back of his career when over-reaching. His hind-shoe had struck into the heel of his front foot. These can be awkward, niggling injuries if they fail to heal quickly.

The over-reach caused a horizontal quarter-crack. James Maine, a partner of Newbury vets, Blackman and O'Gorman, made a good job of it. At the same time Generous suffered a minor bruising to a foot. "We cut out the quarter-crack to prevent it spreading and filled it up with a synthetic hoof filler and then had him shod normally," says James. "If the quarter-crack had been allowed to get bigger it may have been serious. It was the only time I had to deal with Generous throughout his two seasons in training."

It meant Paul could not press on as hard as he perhaps would have liked, so the horse was going to a Classic with a very slightly interrupted preparation. Although the injury did not stop Generous from leaving his box, it prevented him galloping and as a result the final days of his preparation were rushed.

Nevertheless there was enormous stable confidence behind Generous as he went to the General Accident 2,000 Guineas. His trainer who describes himself as "not a big betting man, a £100 each-way occasionally", backed him each-way. Many of the lads staked equal amounts, to win, and several of Whatcombe's other patrons backed the horse as much out of loyalty to the yard as the trainer's confidence.

The race was run on Saturday 4th May 1991. There were 14 runners of which only three, Generous, Mujaazif and Malvernico from Ireland had not already had an outing that season. Marju, the winter favourite, had strengthened his position at the head of the market with a victory in the Craven Stakes, one of the traditionally informative Guineas trials although, back at Arundel where he was trained, they were still not quite sure what to make of the horse. At times he had not worked well in the spring and his performances were to remain something of an enigma throughout the summer. Lester Piggott had the mount on Generous' Dewhurst runner-up Bog Trotter and the Maestro's influence on the race was to play a crucial role. Bog Trotter had won the Greenham at Newbury and as such was another of the fit and fancied brigade. Henry Cecil was to run Desert Sun and Hokusai, the Craven second and third respectively. Desert Sun had, it was believed, come on a great deal for that run.

Of the Newmarket-based runners Mystiko had been an impressive winner of the Free Handicap beating two other runners in the process, Junk Bond and Flying Brave. Mukaddamah, who had beaten Generous at Goodwood as a two-year-old was another but, owned by Hamdam Al Maktoum, was not the choice of his retained jockey Willie Carson who was on board Marju. The French were double handed with André Fabre's Lycius and François Boutin's Ganges.

101

The race provided a popular victory for Lady Beaverbrook's Mystiko trained in Newmarket by Clive Brittain and ridden by Michael Roberts. The grey, on his toes in the parade and taken to the start very slowly by Roberts, had raced on the standside upsides in front. He established a lead three furlongs out when Roberts set sail for home. Mystiko was challenged by Lycius inside the last furlong but stuck his neck out to win in determined style, beating the French raider by a neck. It was his South African jockey's first British Classic.

Ganges led the remainder of the pack home some six lengths away, two and a half lengths in front of Generous who had been outpaced three furlongs out but had really stayed on well up the hill. Mukaddamah was a further five lengths behind him. Marju and Bog Trotter finished well out the back. "He needs a trip," was Richard Quinn's post-race comment.

"The race," comments Paul, "was a bit of a cock-up for me and the rest of the field apart from the first two. Clive Brittain and Michael Roberts had a plan and stuck to it. Most of the others decided they would track Lester in the belief that he was on a good horse. I think on that particular day Bog Trotter wasn't going very well and it was a little bit late before anyone realised what was happening. They all kicked at the same time."

Anthony Penfold was equally adamant that the race had not been run to suit Generous. "I think everyone was mesmerised by Lester and it ended up being two different races within one."

However Generous had shown encouraging signs in the race, he would definitely be suited by further. He had finished fourth despite his preparation and although some of the lads had lost a week's wages on the Guineas they were now highly confident of getting it back at Epsom for which the grey Mystiko, with obvious doubts about his ability to stay, had been installed at the 6–1 favourite. Immediately after the Guineas Generous was 14–1. Equally importantly Generous had behaved well in the parade and had not been stressed by the large crowd.

There is an old saying though: Fourth in the Guineas, First in the Derby.

THE DERBY (part 1)

The Ever Ready Derby is worth, in terms of prize-money to the winner, £355,000, also as soon as the winning colt crosses the line his value as a stallion spirals upwards.

Financially the Derby is no longer the most valuable race run in the world, several others are worth more. And yet, in unquantifiable terms, it remains worth so much more than any other race. It has a prestige and history behind it that make other big races pale into insignificance. When Paul Cole set up in training it was his ambition to win it. When Prince Fahd started owning horses it was his ambition, above all else, to win that particular race. The same is true of jockeys. It remains the ultimate race to win, American owners want to win the British Derby more so than the Kentucky. It is the tops. The Japan Cup, Arc de Triomphe or Breeders' Cup will never take that away from the Epsom Derby.

It takes place on the first Wednesday in June and is run almost a month after the Guineas. A month in racing, as in politics, is a long time and during that time in 1991 much happened.

Generous began to work really well under Tommy Jennings, he continued to work better and better, stronger and stronger. He went to Newbury for a piece of work with three Group/Listed stable companions over a mile and a half. "At the end of the gallop when they were stopping he was just taking off," recalls Paul Cole. "It was very impressive."

It gave the team confidence that Generous would stay

104

the mile and a half trip and that he was a very good horse, win, lose or draw the Derby.

Meanwhile Whatcombe was beginning to enjoy a purple patch with its other runners. Everywhere they went they were not only winning but winning decent races. So often big races are won by stables in form. There was no denying the form and health of the Whatcombe-trained horses approaching 5th June. Later in the season Richard Hannon was quoted as saying that even his stable cat looked like winning a race because his horses were in such good form. The same was true of Whatcombe at the end of May and into early June.

There had, of course, been other significant trials during that month which had seen other colts put forward as suitable Derby-winning candidates, and, of course, a number of previously fancied horses cracked under the pressure that is applied when they are being trained for the Blue Riband. Even Mystiko, until then the favourite, had his foot in a poultice two days before the race. Meanwhile Generous, despite his distinctive colouring which would make him easy to pick out in the race, had failed to catch the public's imagination. Fourth in the Guineas had not been eye-catching enough for the majority.

Within a week of the Guineas though there came about a major change in the Generous camp. On Friday 10th May it was announced that the up-and-coming 24-year-old Alan Munro had been signed up as retained jockey for Prince Fahd. Alan had only known about a possible retainer with the Prince when his business manager, Maurice Hale, had rung him the previous Tuesday as he drove back from Chester races. It was an offer few jockeys could refuse, not least of all Alan who had still been claiming at the start of the 1990 season.

At the time of his selection, a choice made entirely by Prince Fahd, Alan was in his second season as a retained jockey for Newmarket handler Bill O'Gorman. "There was," says Alan, "no reason why Bill should let me go. It was typical of him to say he thought it was in my best interests to accept the job and wish me luck. I was sad to leave and grateful for all he had done."

Initially the signing meant that Alan would ride Ausherra in the following day's Lingfield Oaks Trial but ultimately it meant he would have the ride on Generous in the Derby. It was tough on Richard Quinn who had done a lot of the work with Generous. The public, like they do in some divorce cases, naturally took sides with Richard who it seemed to most was being a little hard done by. He had, after all, ridden Generous in all but one of his seven races and had won three of them including the Group 1 Dewhurst. But Richard himself, although clearly disappointed that many of the rides he had been looking forward to were not going to be his that season, including Generous, accepted the situation with dignity and made little of it. The fact that he went on to have his best season numerically without Prince Fahd's horses was to demonstrate his resilience.

"Life is full of these little things," he said, "but life must go on." It did all seem a little unfair. Richard had after all won two Irish Classics for Prince Fahd the previous season in Knight's Baroness (the Oaks) and Ibn Bey (St Leger).

"These things always seem to happen when you seem to be going so well. I shall keep riding for the stable, keep my head down and keep on punching." It was precisely what he did and his attitude earned him a great deal of respect.

The subject of jockeys remained a 'touchy' subject with Anthony Penfold. For some time afterwards he twitched at the mention of it, it was the only blemish on what was otherwise considered a near-perfect Derby day for the Generous team. "Richard had ridden a lot of big winners for us," he says.

In the 1988 Irish Derby Insan was beaten by the

106

narrowest of margins by Kahyasi after Richard had had his stick knocked out of his hand. It was definitely knocked out of his hand rather than dropped because it went up in the air before falling. It may not have made much differ-ence and, as we all know, the difference between a brilliant ride and an ordinary ride can be very fine, but it nevertheless sowed the seeds of doubt in Prince Fahd's mind. Richard is a fine horseman, in those terms probably finer than Alan, but he has never been as fashionable as Eddery or Carson. He has a lower profile and Prince Fahd, no doubt, had a few people niggling at him, questioning whether he employed the best jockey.

Richard had been jocked off before, from Broken Hearted in the Sussex Stakes and Ibn Bey in the Jockey Club Stakes but on neither occasion did the replacements do any better.

"I don't think Prince Fahd thought Richard gave Generous an outstanding ride in the Guineas," says Anthony. "Some other big owners, the Maktoums for example, retained their own jockeys, Carson and Cauthen, and Prince Fahd's father-in-law retained Pat Eddery. He felt he would rather have his own jockey whom he could use whenever one of his horses ran, from whichever stable, rather than the stable jockey who might be on call elsewhere."

Although Alan's rise towards the top had been nothing if not meteoric, and this deal clinched it. He had been a struggling apprentice with Barry Hills from 1984 until 1986. He had been one of a number of hopefuls hoping to make it at Manton. In three seasons he had managed only one winner, Sentimental Roses, at Yarmouth on 21st August 1985. However kind a critic you could not say his career was going swimmingly, far from it.

However as he proved in 1991 Alan is determined and dedicated. He moved back up north from whence he had come to Mel Brittain's yard at Warthill near York. An incident at Beverley on Hot Ruler in 1986 did much to change his career. The stewards, as they occasionally do to apprentices or inexperienced amateurs, took him to one side and showed him the camera patrol film of the race. It made him wince. It was all the spur that he needed.

His confidence grew. Brittain runs his horses regularly and he was able to get much practice and he took himself off to the United States in the close-seasons to seek further improvement. There, with the help of jockey Lyndon Hanigan he soon developed his distinctive 'American' style. It is now his trade mark.

At the end of the 1989 season he had, with Brittain's backing, established himself as one of the leading apprentices but at the end of the year he was offered the opportunity to move to Newmarket for Bill O'Gorman where he would have first retainer the following summer. In the north Lynda Ramsden was keen to offer him a second retainer.

It was his low-crouching whip-up style on a horse that continued to attract attention in that first season with O'Gorman. It began in whirlwind fashion by his winning the Lincoln on Jimmy Fitzgerald's Evichstar. He rode two other winners at Doncaster's opening meeting and another five before the end of March. The season continued in a similar pattern, Mac's Imp providing the quality by winning the Coventry Stakes and thus providing his first Royal Ascot winner, and Timeless Times providing success on a numerical basis. Together he and the two-year-old colt won 16 races.

However that good season ended prematurely in near disaster. He had ridden 95 winners and was in sight of his first century when, on 30th October, the horse he was riding in the Daily Telegraph Racecall Nursery stumbled, he fell off and only regained consciousness as he was stretchered into a local hospital. He had been kicked 'all over the track' and was lucky to have escaped so lightly.

108

The fall was to keep him off a horse for three months and off the racecourse for longer.

He made his comeback at lowly Southwell on the all weather in February. By May he had been signed up to ride for Prince Fahd and anticipated an even better season.

The retainer could not have got off to a smoother start that is for sure. Ausherra won the next day at Lingfield. At Kempton the following week he made it four wins from four rides for Prince Fahd. It continued until 23rd May when he made his first error. It nearly cost him the Derby ride on Generous when he picked up a four day suspension for careless riding on Magic Ring in a graduation race. The ban was to run from 1st–4th June inclusive making Derby-day his first back in the saddle following the suspension. Many racegoers at Goodwood that day agreed that Alan had been lucky to get away with the minimum sentence for the offence, only four days.

Before Epsom Alan had sat on Generous only a couple of times in canters up Woolley Down. "It did not matter," says Alan reflecting his association with Generous at the end of the summer, "that I had not ridden him much. He was a most uncomplicated horse to ride, not like Suave Dancer who you had to time a late run with. Generous was the sort of horse you could do what you liked with."

Alan had done his homework on Epsom. He sought advice from Lester Piggott's father Keith while serving his ban. He studied videos of Lester's victories around the track. The same tactic had worked for Ray Cochrane in 1988.

The opposition as it always does on paper before a big race looked hot. "There are always two races for the Derby," says Paul Cole, "the one you read about in the papers beforehand, and the one on the day. The papers can make out a case for nearly every horse but when you study a picture of the finish after the race you invariably see them strung out over two furlongs. Some are not sound, some have not got the trip, some have not acted on the track. In Generous we had a horse who had speed, stayed, and would handle the track.

"I told Alan to jump him out in a positive fashion, don't hang about, attack the race, he has speed, balance, acceleration, stays. You've got no problems. The only problems would be created by an extreme of tactic, either making the running or staying covered up at the back like Dancing Brave."

There were a total of 13 runners for the 1991 Ever Ready Derby, Arokat under Paul Eddery pacemaking for the French runner Toulon under Paul's brother Pat. Toulon had been beaten by Suave Dancer first time out but had looked impressive when winning the Chester Vase. Corrupt, whom Generous had beaten on a bad day at Goodwood as a two-year-old, was unbeaten in two outings. He had beaten Environment Friend and subsequently won the Lingfield Trial. He was being partnered by Cash Asmussen who was fresh from his French Derby victory on Suave Dancer three days earlier. Environment Friend would provide a popular victory for George Duffield and young trainer James Fanshawe. He had put his early season form behind him when winning the Dante Stakes at York in another good trial. Sheikh Mohammed, without a Derby success as yet despite considerable investment in bloodstock, was represented by Hailsham, regarded at home as inferior to the Guineas victor Mystiko, whose free style of running appeared unsuited to Epsom's mile and a half. If Toulon was guaranteed to get the trip, the other French challenger, Hector Protector was not. However he had been the Champion European Two-year-old, had won the French 2,000 Guineas and was unbeaten in eight races. He could not be discounted. Lester Piggott was to ride Hokusai who, following a disappointing run in the Guineas had finished fourth in France and appeared to be running as something of an afterthought. Paul Kelleway

110

was bullish about the chances of big outsider Hundra if no one else was. Marju was the unknown quantity. He had proved himself in the Craven but finished lame in the Guineas. His preparation had not been ideal and he had only been a definite runner following his workout the previous Saturday. Mujaazif was another 'iffy' runner. He had injured his back in the Guineas in which he had finished last.

There was one Irish runner, Jim Bolger's Star of Gdansk who had finished second in the Irish Guineas.

THE DERBY DIARY

About three weeks before the Derby Michael Harris, Editor of *The Racing Post* asked me to find a runner in the race which we could follow for a week beforehand on a daily-diary basis.

It would not only give an insider's view on how the horse was trained during that last important week but it would give an insight to the atmosphere within the yard and how some of the people, other than the trainer, were reacting to the impending excitement.

I believe the idea arose principally because Mystiko was running in the race. Mystiko was not only the favourite but trained by Clive Brittain, generally regarded as the most open trainer in British racing and, from the point-of-view of quotes, a journalist's dream.

However I shall be eternally grateful to Clive for turning me down. By the time I got round to ringing I think nearly every newspaper in the kingdom, and several from outside it, had requested an interview with him and Mystiko. But it was, nevertheless, one of the great surprises of my journalistic career that my request was met with a negative answer.

The search had to go elsewhere. James Fanshawe had Environment Friend in the race, but being a second season trainer, was under enough stress without having me under his feet for a week. France, we could go there possibly, I had once ridden a winner for François Boutin and thought I might get a favourable reply from Le Mont de Po, Lamorlaye. However it would be a costly exercise and we did not ask.

The logical horse to write about would be Generous, not only local to my home but he had, after the Guineas, an obvious chance without actually being favourite for the race. Paul Cole, to whom I am grateful for all his help throughout the summer, agreed to let me loose in Whatcombe. Anthony Penfold, another tremendous help, was promptly told by a superstitious friend that any chance Generous had in the race had gone out of the window the moment Generous' preparation had become the subject of a daily diary in *The Racing Post*. Apart from anything else I hope the Derby Diary buried that ghost for good. It was one of the most gratifying moments of my day at Epsom when one of Clive Brittain's lads came up to me following the Derby. "Can you do one of our horses next year?" he asked.

We tried with Generous again before the Arc and I, for one, as you will no doubt feel from the pieces, was convinced lightning would strike twice.

Derby Diary: Wednesday, 29th May, 1991

GENEROUS, the Guineas fourth, stands patiently in his box. Brushed over, he awaits work rider Tommy Jennings' saddle. Rubber and under-saddle pads in place, the Caerleon colt decides it's time to stretch, upsetting his rider's careful placement. Jennings curses and has to start again.

"A bag of muscles," he comments, giving Generous a hearty slap on the ribs. Generous, fit and hard, doesn't even flinch. A fly landing on him would have caused more irritation.

Seven days before the Derby and Generous, whose two-year-old season culminated in his winning the Dewhurst Stakes, is due to have a good blow-out over a mile and a furlong up Woolley Down. There's not a gallop as stiff as this within 50 miles of Newmarket where Mystiko, the horse the yard believes will be the biggest danger, is trained.

The chestnut colt, a workwatcher's dream with a distinguished blond mane and 'highlighted' tail — which has earned him the nickname 'Grundy' — is laid back, switched off, but that hasn't always been the case.

He's a gentleman in his box too, not at all colty like you might expect. He doesn't try to take a chunk out of you if you get too close to his head and he doesn't raise his hind feet in threat if you're busy at the other end. One of his stablemates proved to be too colty during first lot and attacked Richard Quinn, wrestling the jockey to the ground. On the way home, he kicked another lad. By breakfast that colt was on his way to the vet's. Generous, with the manners of a gelding, knows there are pleasanter ways of spending breakfast!

Pulled out at 7.30 am, he walks round in the main yard with 35 others, attentive and alert while trainer Paul Cole dishes out each lad's orders.

Soon he is trotting briskly up the lane to South Fawley. Eight deer crash through the undergrowth of the hedge before watching the string from the comparative safety of a wheat field. Generous is unperturbed by what several other horses use as an excuse to display their well-being.

Woolley Down is ascended once at the canter and, second time, at a somewhat swifter pace. Alan Munro leads him by a couple of lengths on Affair Of Honour, also owned by Prince Fahd Salman, whose racing manager, Anthony Penfold, is on hand to see the blow-out. They go a steady halfspeed before Jennings joins and passes his lead sprinting clear over the last furlong and a half. It was just what was required.

He walks home quietly, neither sweating nor blowing for long. Placid, he even has to give his lead horse a lead past some boisterous bullocks. The brief heatwave we had last week has gone and gloves, put away for the summer, have suddenly been recommissioned.

"A bit drafty," understated Jennings, a work rider of the old school. Formerly a jump jockey, he spent 11 years as second jockey, principally to Willie Robinson, at Fulke Walwyn's.

Jennings has been put on Generous for the last two weeks of his Derby preparation. "I rode Zoman last year and the difference between the two is that this one will definitely get the trip," he explains. "There was always a question mark about Zoman getting it but we are as sure as we can be that this fellow wants a mile and a half. In that respect he's a better prospect for the Derby."

His last serious workout was at Newbury eight days previously with Run Don't Fly, a Group 2 winner in Italy on Saturday, Half A Tick, third in the Italian Derby, and Widyan, who finished a length behind his stable-companion in the same race. The stable is in form. "Generous is in better form now than he was before the Guineas too," adds Jennings.

115

"All's fine with the horse," said Cole later in the morning. Anthony Penfold, who bought Generous at the Cartier Million Sale, touched wood as he said it. "That will have given him confidence. He's learned to settle very well now and there's no prize-money to be won up there on the Downs."

This is not a one-horse-one-race yard, though. Zoman goes to France and Ruby Tiger to Germany at the weekend. Entries have to be discussed and made for Generous for Group races as far off as November. There's plenty to occupy the trainer's mind, and he, like the horse, seems very relaxed about the impending excitement. Penfold, on the other hand, would like to treat it as any other race but is finding it difficult to do so.

But what are the tell-tale signs we should be looking for a week before the big one that indicates that a three-year-old is reaching a peak? Paul Cole knows the answer. "You want to start taking notice," he says, "when Tommy Jennings starts bringing in bundles of grass for the horse after exercise."

No matter that Generous was to spend much of the morning on the bank above the main yard in a circular grazing cage; there was a bundle of grass, a double armful of it, outside his box as Jennings brushed him over following first lot.

Derby Diary: Thursday, 30th May, 1991

THURSDAYS are easy days for the 110 inmates of What-combe, Derby runners included. "Village and One" was the general instruction this morning. Trot up to South Fawley, come back and have one canter up a five-furlong all-weather on the Great Shefford side of the yard.

Generous pleases his work rider Tommy Jennings, not so much because he moves well up the hill but because he's not fizzing following Wednesday's workout. "It's a good sign," he said. "He's still very relaxed. Sometimes you can feel them tensing up the day after work and you know that the pressure is beginning to get to them."

At breakfast the trainer volunteers his first thoughts about his horse and the race. An open-looking contest this year? "Well, not so open as you all think," suggests Paul Cole.

He explained: "The Derby is two races; the one you read about in the papers beforehand and the actual race at Epsom. Next Thursday you will see a head-on photo of the finish in the papers and see them strung out over a furlong.

"It's a fact, every year, that 50 per cent of the trials for the race will be proved meaningless by the actual Derby. Some horses will have been overworked, some will have had troubled preparations, some won't have acted round Epsom.

"Training a Derby winner is like baking a good cake: you need all the right ingredients. We thought we had most of them last year with Zoman, although we knew there was a doubt about his staying the trip. I think we have most of the ingredients this time. We're more confident about Generous staying the trip, he'll act there, he's sound, he's a fresh horse and he's going forward.

"And," adds Cole, "Generous is in very safe hands." He's referring to Robert Latham, the colt's lad. Loyal and hard-working, the 24-year-old has been with Cole for nine years now. He joined two days after leaving school.

Few people will ever get to know Generous as well as he does — perhaps only the stallion man, if he ends up at stud. You'd like the horse to win just because you know how much it would mean to Latham.

"This is the top for a stable lad, as high as you can go, to do the winner of the Derby. It means everything," he says.

Latham hasn't had a penny on Generous. "I can't afford to lose," he says, not even regretting the fact that he didn't back Generous at 50–1 in the Dewhurst. Some of his colleagues who lost £50 in the Guineas will go in twice as heavy this time trying to recoup the loss. It is the mentality that keeps most bookmakers in profit and many lads on the breadline.

Latham arrives for afternoon stables at 4pm. He looks after three other horses but attends to Generous first. It takes him roughly 35 minutes to muck out, hay and water, and brush the colt over. Having finished him, he will let him down but will have him back on parade when the trainer looks round at 5.30.

"He's very quiet to look after, no vices," says Latham. "Quiet to ride and quiet to do." Until Jennings took over recently, he rode Generous out every day. "He also gets a branch of horse-chestnut leaves during evening stables. Some horses don't like them but there's plenty of iron in them and he can play with the branch to keep him occupied." Colts need amusing.

But Generous' temperament has not always been so easy-going. "The third time he ran last year was at Goodwood and it was a very hot day," recalls Latham. "He had to be washed down four times to keep cool. We were very disappointed with his run. He was beginning to get worse in his box at home and things were getting to him.

118

"He's not a great sleeper at the best of times and when he went to Deauville for his next outing he was in stables next to the sales ring. So after the noise of the racing during the day he was kept awake by the tannoy of the sales at night. It was driving him mad. He ran badly despite our high expectations."

Generous could have gone the wrong way from that point but Cole decided to give him three weeks out at grass in the cages on the bank above the yard. "He wasn't totally let down," remembers Latham, "but as good as. He came back fantastic after that, though, and was back to being a gent in his box again.

"The guv'nor then found a very easy race for him at Sandown which was like a piece of work. That was ideal; it gave him his confidence back."

In his box, Generous is talking to his neighbour Zoman. "They're daft about each other," says Latham. "They always eat together and if one leaves his manger the other will too. Zoman's on shavings because he eats his bed. I think Generous passes him straw from his own bed through the bars: they're the best of pals!"

Derby Diary: Friday, 31st May, 1991

TWENTY-FIVE horses dot the bank alongside the What-combe drive, like the cavalry taking a break from a long journey. Generous stands picking at knee-length grass, Tommy Jennings making sure the colt doesn't tread on his reins as he eats.

Generous is very relaxed; he wouldn't have gone far if he'd been let loose. Peaceful — you won't get a greater contrast than this and the helter-skelter of Epsom on Derby Day.

After Thursday's quiet day, though, the whole place seems busier now. Head lad Colin Ratcliffe is normally first in at 5.30am, when he feeds each horse the best part of a bowl of oats. Not today. Ruby Tiger left for Baden-Baden at 2am. Less than two hours later Zoman, next door to Generous, was being prepared for his 4am start for France. The two Nottingham runners are leaving at the more civilised time of 9am.

In the office, secretaries Di and Liz are preparing wage packets. Liz, wife of jockey Chris Rutter, also has to confirm Generous' Derby entry before noon. She says: "Last year, Mr Cole was in and out every five minutes reminding me to confirm Zoman. He seems more relaxed this time." She rings Weatherbys, giving the yard's code, quotes Generous' entry code and the job is done.

Generous has had two canters today up the shavings all-weather. After one steady one, he strode on a second time up. It's a handy gallop, close to the yard, on the collar all the way; you could get horses pretty fit here without having to go to Woolley Down.

Having had his pick of grass, Generous is led back to his box, all the while trying to steal grass from the bundle under Jennings' arm. The work rider wouldn't look out of place at a flower show with all the greenery he's carrying.

The big decision the trainer has to make today is what to

do with Generous tomorrow. Eating an exotic-looking, rancid-smelling Sun Fish for breakfast, Paul Cole chews over both problems, the fish and Generous.

"There are two choices really. Either I take him to the grass on Woolley Down and give him some work where he'd pass a lead horse. That would really be more of a reassuring gallop for the trainer than the horse. He's pretty fit, though, and I don't want to overdo him.

"The alternative is to keep to the all-weather. Three days up the all-weather would be the same as giving him a good workout and Sunday off."

He weighs up the pros and cons. The morning's headlines are about Guy Harwood's dashed Derby hopes — a reminder about the dangers of a serious workout on turf at this stage.

"We've had three dry summers and it might be chancing it even on Woolley now. The all-weather is safer and probably better for him mentally. We got our best big horses, Snurge and Ibn Bey, fit on it alone last year. They were too heavy to go pounding up the turf."

He will also be influenced by Generous' weight. If he is heavy a more serious gallop might be in order. Decisions.

Cole didn't quite finish the fish. At the other end of the breakfast table his assistant Rupert Arnold 'licked his manger clean', leaving only a pile of fish-bones and no flesh on his plate.

Generous has also been eating well lately. At 7am Ratcliffe had checked his manger, and there was not an oat left after his breakfast. Generous has obviously not been upset by the nocturnal movements of horses, people and horseboxes.

"He's a pretty good doer," says Ratcliffe, 16 years Cole's head lad. "He's not fed any different from a selling plater, mind you. He get about 16lb of oats a day with a bit of beet pulp, bran, nuts and oat balancer (maize, peas and molasses mix) thrown in."

All head lads have little additives, a powder here and a herb there. Ratcliffe is no different but they're secrets Ratcliffe wants to keep. "You wouldn't know if they work, though," he adds before moving on.

"Generous' main meal is his supper, fed at the end of evening stables. Breakfast and lunch are basically snacks. The main art is to keep them on their grub. If you tried to give him an extra bowl of oats just because he's running in the Derby he'd probably go off his grub and take two days to get back on it. You can't go experimenting like that a week before the Derby.

"During the winter Generous will have had less food and I've built it up as he's started doing more work. If you overfeed in the winter you've got nothing to work on in the summer."

Generous is given four slabs of Canadian hay a day, although he probably only eats two. It's the big idle colts not doing a lot who will eat all four slabs.

"Horses are deceiving," adds Ratcliffe, who dishes up an old-fashioned 'branmash' on Saturday evenings. "Ibn Bey was an enormous horse but didn't have much of an appetite; smaller horses are often better doers."

Shy of the stalking cameramen who have come to see Generous, Ratcliffe — head lad, witch doctor, medicine man, equine chef, call him what you will — dives off to meet the visiting vet. The horses have been doing the talking for Colin Ratcliffe for a long time now and he's happier to leave it that way.

Derby Diary:
Saturday and Sunday, 1st and 2nd June, 1991

ROBERT Latham, Generous' lad, fork and muck-sack in hand, yawns as he strolls across the yard. He's entitled to, having spent six hours on security the previous night. No trip to the local with the other lads, fresh pay-packets in their pockets. No night out for the missus. Instead she brings his supper out to him in the yard.

Still, Latham doesn't mind, he's paid for it and he hasn't got a thumping head to remind him of the previous night's activities like some of his colleagues.

Paul Cole's gone the way he suggested he would on Friday and decided to give Generous three goes up the five-furlong all-weather.

Generous and Affair of Honour, ridden by Alan Munro, hack up together the first time, stride on the second time and do a good bit the third time. Affair Of Honour is not so much a lead horse as company for Generous. They walk quietly in at the bottom of the gallop each time, quieter than most steeplechasers would. And the pair take no notice of stable companions working past them as they return to the bottom again.

The Whatcombe team may have a more worried, edgy, less relaxed Generous on Wednesday but there seems no doubt that they have achieved one of their principal aims with the horse, whose ability on the racecourse was twice affected adversely by the state of his mind as a two-year-old.

The trainer on his grey hack checks that's all well as the two chestnuts return from their third spin. "I suppose you ought to come and sit on him on Monday," he says to Munro. It all seems so casual, the way he supposes, but you know it's an order with which Munro won't argue. The jockey, his name embroidered on the back of his jacket, has ridden him twice before at home but once more wouldn't do either him or the horse any harm.

PHOTOGRAPH CAPTIONS
PAGES 125–128

Page 125

Alan Munro talks to Anthony Penfold before Generous was galloped at Newbury Racecourse before racing on Saturday 21st September two weeks and one day before the Arc. Alan rode Generous' pacemaker in the gallop.

Page 126

A fine study of Tommy Jennings and Generous by the racing photographer Edward Whittaker as he finishes well ahead of his pacemaker at Newbury.

Generous looked a superb specimen of a classic middle distance thoroughbred that day and raised many hopes for a successful trip to Paris.

Page 127

Arc day at Longchamp, Paul Cole and his wife Vanessa photographed on the stands surrounding the parade ring before one of the preliminary races.

Page 128

After the Arc, Prince Fahd pats a shocked Alan Munro's shoulder in a most sporting gesture.

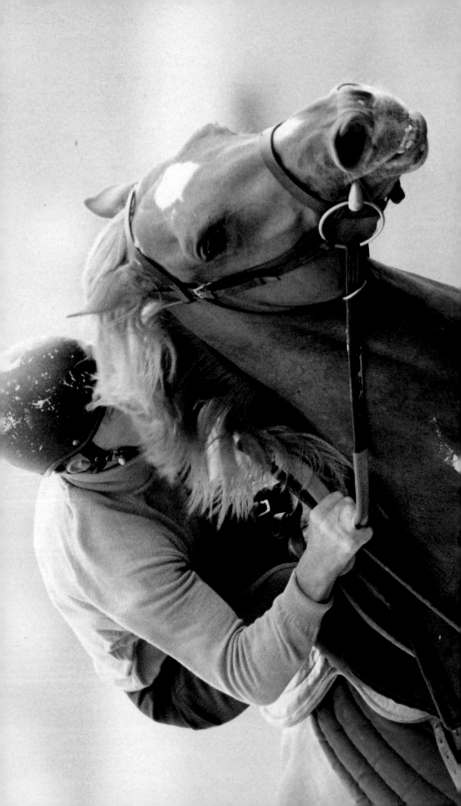

Cod roe on toast is altogether more acceptable than Asian fish. Breakfast in the house for the dozen or so odds and sods who breeze in from the yard is spent looking at the television. While Cole was supervising Generous on the all-weather his wife Vanessa was videoing the work on Woolley Down, the ultimate in DIY SIS.

It's not a pessimist's toy though. The camcorder makes the workers look like they can only crawl and the Richard Attenborough on the other end of it also has very shaky hands. But with some refinement and a tripod, Mrs Cole's enterprise could mean that trainers not only don't have to go racing, with satellites beaming it into their sitting rooms, they won't even have to go up on to the gallops!

Later the Morning Line's discussion on Derby form prompts the trainer to recall Generous' Newbury gallop as the horse's best form line. Munro and Richard Quinn, who both rode in the gallop, agree. "The form of that gallop looks very good," he says. "They went a mile and a half, Run Don't Fly, Half A Tick and Widyan, and Generous was pulling hard in behind them." All three have since acquitted themselves well in Italy. The jockeys agree it was a testing gallop.

"Tomorrow," says Cole, by now with Canadian honey on his toast, "Generous'll go up Woolley Down. He's doing so well and eating everything put in front of him; we'll give him a good canter." By then Cole will be on a private plane to Chantilly.

Munro, beginning a four-day ban for careless riding — the penny now dropped over who the lads referred to when they talked of 'Tinopener' and 'Moses' — had driven down to Hungerford after riding at Hamilton, getting there just before midnight. The driving's the one aspect of a jockey's living that no-one envies.

"I'm trying to treat it as a normal race," he says, talking about the Derby. "So far it's working." His two sits on Generous have been in light work only. "Obviously I'm familiar with all his races and I actually rode against him when he won first time up at Ascot last year."

Based in Cambridge but spending two nights a week in Hungerford, Munro rode Paul Kelleway's Sober Mind in the Derby last year. "It was a 200–1 shot but we beat the favourite Razeen, that's my claim to fame."

Sunday's no day of rest. A sizeable team, including Zoman's work-rider, have gathered for the Channel hop to Chantilly. After a cold week it's altogether more like summer, more like June. Although cricketers would still want a jumper on in the outfield the temperature is markedly up. Relief for the fillies although it won't make much difference to Generous or the colts. In fact a heat-wave on Wednesday is not what the doctor's ordering for Generous.

On Thursday Jennings had asked Cole if he was needed on Sunday. The trainer suggested they should take things "one day at a time," but Jennings is there on duty.

Five furlongs up Woolley and not even a girth mark on the colt when he returns. The plan is falling smoothly into shape.

Derby Diary: Monday, 3rd June, 1991

THIS week has started well, or last week ended well, whichever way you look at it.

Two continental runners on Sunday netted another £55,000 in marks and francs for Paul Cole's foreign policy. Ruby Tiger, the first horse owned by sculptor Philip Blacker, won a Group 2 in Baden-Baden and Zoman ran Sanglamore to within a length in the Group 1 Prix d'Ispahan at Chantilly.

The spotlight is turning to Wednesday, although the tension of it all is still not being outwardly shown. Two days away and either they're a cool bunch down at Whatcombe or there simply is no tension yet. I suspect it's the former.

It's a lovely morning up on Woolley Down, cool, breezy but bright sunshine. Alan Munro is having his third sit on Generous. The Caerloen colt has a good canter, five furlongs uphill, a length off Affair Of Honour. It's a wonderful picture, two horses striding out over a springy green carpet, a hundred acres to themselves. Munro hops off at the top and Robert Latham gets on Generous for the quiet walk home, along tracks lined with red campion and past fields of linseed.

"That's fantastic," says the trainer at breakfast, delighted that Generous has remained so switched off. Munro, perhaps more experienced on sprinters and precocious types, is almost worried that he's too switched off. "We've been trying to get him like that all summer," reassures Cole. "Don't be worried about it. It's nice to have a horse who you have to ask to do something."

Munro, who has booked an appointment for an eve-of-Derby pep-talk with Lester Piggott, is not fussed at never having ridden Generous in a race before. It's an everyday occurrence for the young jockey. The fact that he's booked in with The Maestro is the first obvious sign that he has the race on his mind.

131

The most outward sign of building excitement is that the Derby is being talked about more and more, in the yard, in the office, at breakfast. "It's changed a lot in the last five or six years," says Cole. "It's not the mad rush and panic that it used to be. It's a colder, more calculated race now.

"The big entry fees mean that fewer hopefuls run and aren't even entered. It's just the professional owners, and it's made it a more clinical race. All the jockeys know what the others will be doing, and it's taken some of the excitement away. There shouldn't be any excuses these days.

"I only enter my probables in the race now. The possibles that I might have entered five years ago get an entry in the French or Italian Derbys."

Generous, his training almost complete, spends the afternoon having the finishing touches applied. More like an actor than athlete, it's time for cosmetics. He has his mane pulled. It won't make him go any faster, and one hopes it won't have the same effect that it had on Samson, but he'll look the part — smart and tidy.

Local blacksmith Alfie Hall takes off his steel training shoes and puts on a pair of aluminium racing plates. He uses an American variety with metal toe inserts so that they last longer. They won't have to come off until next Monday, saving his feet. The fewer times nails are knocked in the better.

"They're a fraction heavier than the pure aluminium ones but not enough to make any difference," says Hall with Generous' ready-made plates in his hand. "He has normal feet and is easy to do, unlike Zoman, who tries to pick you up in his teeth."

Hall, who also shoes for Tim Forster — "In Uncle Merlin I should have shod a Grand National winner last year" — will be at Epsom on Wednesday, a valuable member of Generous' entourage. "We wouldn't go up for a race like the National where the racecourse farrier would re-shoe

132

anything needing it, but you'll find every trainer takes his own blacksmith for the Derby. Hopefully I won't be needed but it's safer to have someone on hand who knows the horse's feet."

It's a day out he and his colleagues, unsung heroes all, will enjoy. He enjoyed going with Zoman last year. "I hope Generous wins. The only time we normally get a mention is when something goes wrong!"

Hall is yet to shoe a Derby winner. He wasn't around when Blakeney and Morston were sent out from Whatcombe by Arthur Budgett to win the 1969 and 1973 Derbys respectively.

The yard has a history of which most establishments would be proud. The box which stabled those two is the only one that wasn't converted and modernised when Cole took over in 1985. A small pokey little one it is with a full door on it.

Whatcombe boasts two other Derby winners, Trigo in 1929 and Blenheim in 1930, heroes from the golden years of Dick Dawson, whose first major winner from Whatcombe was Drogheda in the 1898 Grand National.

There must be ghosts around. In 1935, when Dawson's lads were digging a grave for the stallion Blandford, who stood at Whatcombe, they uncovered the remains of a Saxon village destroyed by the Black Death in the mid-14th century. It's now a protected site.

Blandford only ran four times but sired four Derby winners, including Trigo and Blenheim. One wonders if his fatherly spirit will look down favourably when Generous attempts to add another chapter to the history of this famous combe.

Derby Diary: Tuesday, 4th June, 1991

"IT would be a pity to lose the Derby because of a parrot," says Paul Cole, Master of Whatcombe, master of understatement.

That was it. I knew something had been missing from riding out at Whatcombe this past week. The colourful Amazon called Oscar, responsible for getting more lads dropped than anything else, is no longer allowed to fly during the morning. Like a Stealth bomber he would glide quietly up behind the string as it pulled out of the drive, pick his target, lock on and swoop, screeching at a horse or lad.

Instead, in his peacetime role, he escorts Prince Fahd Salman's car up to the house during the afternoon. Generous' owner had come to discuss the horse and the race. It's becoming an eve-of-Derby tradition for owner and trainer.

Cole has his theories: "Historically they normally set off at a million miles an hour, all get a position, pull up so that they all come round Tattenham Corner in a heap. But with the size of field this year I think you'd be half-baked if you couldn't get a run provided you've got a horse underneath you.

"I'll give Alan three scenarios but I won't tie him down too much. It can only give him a feeling of what might happen."

The Whatcombe team has done all it can now. It just remains for Generous to do his bit and show he has the ability and necessary brilliance to win a Derby. Throw in a bit of luck too.

"He's in great form and mentally he's so well," says Cole, wondering who'll achieve greatest fame: tomorrow's Derby winner or the Ludgrove schoolboy who thwacked Prince William with a golf club. Both will live with it for the rest of their lives. "I can't think of any excuses at this stage. Anything that goes wrong with Generous now can only do so in his box."

For the second morning in succession Generous has a good canter over five furlongs on Woolley Down a length behind a lead. "He loves that work, running away in behind a lead. People don't think horses are intelligent but he loves the fact that he could pick up and pass the lead in a stride if asked."

Tommy Jennings is pleased too. "You haven't seen him do a serious piece of work but he has the ability to win, I'm sure. I'm convinced he'll be in the first three at any rate. He's not a difficult horse to ride, not like Ausherra who runs in the Oaks. Alan Munro won't have any trouble."

Generous' feet are ice-cold after being shod the previous day. Jennings is careful at this stage to avoid walking on flints or stones. The horse has intelligence according to the trainer but even if he were an equine Einstein he'd be hard pushed to imagine what difference a day makes, what he'll be doing at 3.45 pm tomorrow.

Hares, as confused as the rest of us about the time of year, box on Woolley, partridges take dust baths in the dirt canter. Generous looks on interestedly as his stable-companions work up the Down as he wanders home. This is the blissful calm before the storm. "We'll need blinkers on him if we get him any more switched off!" jokes Jennings. "This time last year he'd be in a white lather after that."

Ten pounds better, at least, than he was in the Guineas, that's the work-rider's estimation. He fears Corrupt most of all.

The rest of the day would give Generous little indication of what's about to happen. Perhaps he'll notice the lads getting twitchier, talking faster, more excited, sweaty hands fiddling with their ante-post betting slips. The visit from the Prince.

He takes a pick of grass on the way in, spends an hour

before lunch in a cage, has the same meals as normal. Last year Zoman went to Epsom on the Monday, but not Generous. Any benefit a familiarising canter round Tattenham Corner might do at this stage would only be lost in fretting.

Now we're nearly there we can start worrying about the opposition. Mystiko gets a mention; you can't knock Classic form. Rupert Arnold has scanned the form and says Star Of Gdansk isn't out of it. Colin Ratcliffe has respect for Hector Protector.

The trainer mentions Toulon, but he would have fancied Marju with a less-troubled preparation and he guarantees Corrupt will run well although wonders if he has the brilliance of a Derby winner.

"Our main danger is that the pacemaker won't do his job properly. Ninety per cent of the time they don't." Kind though Khalid Abdullah may be, Arokat, the pacemaker, isn't in for Generous' benefit. "If he doesn't go fast enough and make it a true mile-and-a-half race it will open it up to the mile-and-a-quarter horses and there are plenty of them."

Anthony Penfold, the Prince's racing manager, is as relaxed as could be expected. "Obviously it's a big day," he says, "but there's nothing Prince Fahd or myself can do now except worry!

"Personally I respect both of the Guineas winners. If one of them stays it has to be our biggest danger. If Vincent O'Brien's theory that you can win the Derby with a good mile-and-a-quarter horse is right, then who knows?"

It's all conjecture, though, and in 24 hours all our theories will be of no consequence. Generous, athlete and equine brainbox, take a lesson from the parrot and swoop to conquer. It's all in your hands now.

Derby Diary: Wednesday, 5th June, 1991

GENEROUS stands in a straw box, one of the many in Epsom's Racecourse Stables. Robert Latham holds the Grundy look-alike — now Grundy race-alike — in his racing bridle. A man shuffles the straw. Latham whistles. The indignity of it all.

No longer in-waiting, Generous is now the king owned by a prince. He's just run the race of his life, beaten the best in the style of a champion. He's just added a nought to his value, Ir£200,000 at purchase, and maybe more. And now he stands in a dope box, being watched by some of his entourage, as they wait for him to have a pee. No privacy. It's a miracle in the circumstances that it only takes him five minutes to get the urge.

"It's taken nothing out him," says Latham, still not regretting the fact that he didn't back him in the Dewhurst, and not fussed about not investing this time either. Just doing the Derby winner is good enough for him. It's little use talking to him. He's up in the clouds.

An hour later Generous is padded up to make the victorious journey back to Whatcombe. It's unlikely he will ever do a better day's work.

The Derby winner's day began at 5.00 am, awoken by the sound of head lad Colin Ratcliffe flipping the latches back on the stable doors as he rushed round with breakfast. Three-parts of a bowl of oats. It's a chilly, quiet, morning at Whatcombe. The last lad in charge of Generous' security knocks off as Ratcliffe feeds him.

Latham, in half an hour earlier than usual, does little to Generous. He won the best-turned-out for the 2,000 Guineas by doing little to Generous. It won't make him run faster and the more he does to him the more it is likely to wind him up. Travelling boots on, tail bandaged, Generous loaded; Paul Cole's box, a giant six-pack, glides out of Whatcombe as the stragglers arrive to tack up in time for first lot. And so to Epsom.

The trainer is relaxed, Vanessa Cole even more so. It's only the Prince's racing manager Anthony Penfold who is giving cause for concern. If he were a horse he'd be confined to the swimming pool. Mrs Cole also points out that he'd probably have been cut by now. He's definitely the most nervous member of the party. Don't let him near Generous, who hasn't turned a hair.

Penfold chats a lot, says he's not nervous a lot—always a bad sign, that. He stabs himself with a staple from his racecard and admits that even his dog has been getting geed up these last few days. They are nervous moments, though maybe Cole just hides it better.

Latham spends a quarter of an hour brushing Generous over before pulling him out of the racecourse yard. The colt is one of the few who is plaited. He walks round the paddock, not even warm. At 494kg of hard racehorse, he's 5kg lighter than he was for the Guineas. Munro is riding a winner for Clive Brittain at the same time. A good sign. The day has started well.

"We've been here before and we've been stuffed," says Cole as he walks in to pick up Munro's saddle. Famous last words. "If you had the guts you'd tell your jockey to come up the stand side," he comments. It's firm where he walks down to the saddling boxes. Generous is still calm and hasn't turned a hair, not even Paul Kelleway flapping his top hat to get Hundra in a box can upset him.

Chamois, pad, number-cloth, saddle. He's saddled in two minutes, his muscles shaking, he nudges Latham a few times before settling down to take an interest in the other horses. Ears pricked, Cole's plan to keep him relaxed has worked. It's only when he comes out on to the course to parade that he gets a bit damp down his neck. Hokusai's damper. He's on his toes now but Mystiko more so.

138

The trainer watches from the Prince's box, Latham from outside the weighing room where he can see a television, work-rider Tommy Jennings at home in Lambourn, the whole yard gathered round a box in the hostel.

The race, well, you'll read about that elsewhere. Perfectly placed throughout but he won that well it probably didn't matter. In the press box afterwards Paul Cole's smile says more than words. It's always the case on these occasions. Anthony Penfold? You'd never think he'd been nervous at all. Perhaps his dog will relax now.

Generous . . . well, he'll have been tucked up in bed, not edgy or jumpy as we thought he might be, when most of Whatcombe move two miles down the road to The Swan, Great Shefford. "There'll be a few free drinks down there I'd think," says Tommy Jennings.

You'd hope the Prince picks up this tab.

THE DERBY (part II)

Epsom 5th June 1991. A cold breezy day, a smaller crowd than usual, the back of the grandstands, in the process of being rebuilt, looking more like a bombsite. Was the Derby about to lose some of its glamour? It was going to need a scintillating victory if people were going to go home with the race etched on their minds instead of the rather chilly day.

Prince Fahd was at the Derby with a cousin whom he had been brought up with. He had been in the paddock and decided to leave and go back to the stands in time to see the horses parade and canter back past the stables to the start. The pair made a dash for it, the fitter Prince striding out, his friend having trouble laying up with the pace.

However, as they left the paddock the clerk of the course, Michael Webster, asked if they would be kind enough to wait a couple of minutes to allow the Queen to pass by. Prince Fahd had been hoping to avoid any hold ups.

"We waited for the Queen and her Mother to pass and we walked back on the racecourse towards the stands," says Prince Fahd, recalling one of his favourite Derby stories. "When we got to the little gate in front of the winning line to enter the stands there was a lady standing in front of me. That lady happened to be the Queen Mother. I couldn't go through unless I tapped her on the shoulder and said 'excuse me' and I did not feel it quite appropriate for me to do that. Now the person who witnessed this was the Queen herself. She came over to her Mother and said, 'There are people behind you' and the Queen Mother walked away. But the Queen came to me and said: 'Good luck with your horse.' And I took off my hat and was overwhelmed by her statement and shook hands with her immediately. I probably wasn't supposed to but it happened so quickly.

"Then I went up to my box with Prince Khalid, whose box was next to mine, and said: 'I just shook hands with the Queen and this is what she said to me.' He replied that one was supposed to shake hands with the Queen after the race not before. I said maybe before and after!"

"I don't want to go over the top about the horse," says Alan Munro reflecting on his season with Generous, "but his response was electrifying when I asked him to quicken in the Derby. When Mystiko and the pacemaker died away, he hit the front with his ears pricked. I was not expecting any response when another horse came into my view but he just took off when I asked. This shouldn't happen to myself at the time."

The Derby ended Alan's fairytale first month as Prince Fahd's jockey on a high note although the ensuing half an hour following the race was to turn into something of a nightmare as his confidence in the post-race press conference was taken for arrogance and cockiness.

The starter checked that all jockeys were happy. In a central London branch of William Hill, one out-of-breath punter scattered the gathered crowd in the shop and laid £5,000 in notes, on the cashier's desk. "Two and a half grand each-way on Generous." He was just in time. Back at Epsom an eager crowd waited in the stands and on the downs. The starter rechecked his watch, 3.46 pm, a minute late, and with a brief warning "Okay Jockeys," he pulled the trigger that automatically opened the stalls.

They were off and across Epsom an excited buzz went up much like it does at Aintree when they set off in the Grand National.

141

After a reasonably level break the 13 runners set off uphill towards the first slight right-handed dog's leg. They had gone fully a quarter of a mile before they had begun to sort themselves out. On the good to firm but spongy turf Michael Roberts was setting a tremendous gallop on Mystiko; the 2,000 Guineas winner's keen style of running was to prove fruitless over the Derby trip. He was even a length up on the hard ridden pacemaker Arokat at this early stage with Generous back in fourth just behind and to the outside of Hokusai and Lester, another just off the early pace on the rails. Close behind this pair were Star of Gdansk and Hector Protector while the remainder of the closely grouped field was being whipped in by the outsider Hundra.

Another two furlongs on, up towards the highest point of the course and Mystiko still led Arokat who had tried and failed to get to the front. The pair were taking each other on up the hill and were to pay the consequences, both dropping out suddenly after they had gone a mile. In behind, the fast gallop was suiting Generous very well, his high cruising speed allowing him to keep the leading pair well within his sights. He was poised, going easily.

So placed, the runners for the 1991 Derby began the long swoop into Tattenham Corner, the shape of the race having changed remarkably little. It was not until they had emerged from the awkward, unbalancing bend that the picture began to alter dramatically. Generous had travelled the famous, steep, uncambered corner in good style, and in a clear third place suffering no interference or sandwiching from other less balanced colts. Behind him Hokusai still had the rail, Hector Protector was one off the rail on his outer struggling with the camber, Steve Cauthen had moved Hailsham into a challenging position. Behind these three Marju was making his way along the rail, Willie Carson getting him to within striking distance. On his outer Star of Gdansk and Corrupt, behind them, Hundra making progress from the rear and the grey

Environment Friend not travelling so well. Behind him Toulon and already tailed off Mujaazif.

As they straightened up for home Mystiko came to the end of his tether and stopped quickly. Arokat had already begun to drop out. It was here that Alan took the bull by the horns and took it up on Generous. There was rarely a moment of doubt about the result once Alan had engaged overdrive two and a half furlongs out. Behind him Marju had slipped through up the rails but took a few strides to get into top gear. Hector Protector tried to go with him for a while but eventually his class gave best to his lack of stamina. On his outside Star of Gdansk was staying on. The further they went, however, the more obvious the winner. Inside the final furlong Alan gave Generous four cracks to keep him up to his work. At the line Alan registered his delight with a punch in the air; he had five lengths to spare over Marju who, in turn, was seven in front of Star of Gdansk. A half length back came Hector Protector who short-headed the gallant Hundra, who had been impeded, for fourth. Corrupt was next with Hokusai, failing to provide Lester with his 10th Derby, in seventh. The rest were strung out, as Paul Cole had predicted, over the best part of a furlong.

Excuses? You would need a good one for it to wear. Willie Carson was delighted with Marju considering his preparation. Christy Roche had not had the clearest of runs on Star of Gdansk stuck in behind Hector Protector coming down the hill but had stayed on rather than showing any blistering turn of foot. Freddie Head on Hector Protector had tried to go with the winner, he said, but had clearly not stayed. Hundra, said Bruce Raymond, might have been fourth had he not been impeded by Hokusai who had failed to get the last furlong. Cash Asmussen, who had won the French Derby on the previous Sunday, reported that Corrupt had been in the right place at the right time but had been unable to quicken.

Steve Cauthen had always been bustling Hailsham along and Toulon was, according to Pat Eddery, never going. The same applied to Environment Friend.

Generous' time for the mile and a half was 2 m 34.00 s. He had clocked a time only 0.16 outside Kahyasi's electrically timed record. The time of a race like the Derby though is insignificant, that did not matter. What did, was the style in which Generous, a 9–1 shot, had annihilated the rest of the field.

"He was way above anything I've ever ridden," says Alan. "It was my first taste and a big leap up the ladder and, unlike someone like Pat Eddery, I haven't had that many to compare him to, but if I ever get another like him I'll be an exceptionally lucky man. I feel privileged to have ridden him. The great thing about him in the Derby, and his other races for that matter, was that he was such an uncomplicated horse to ride."

Back at Whatcombe evening stables were delayed by the euphoric lads. The local bookmaker, Stan James, was not a happy bookie with £50,000 to pay out, much of it to the lads. Corals, Ladbrokes and William Hill all described the result as a good race for them. Wally Pyrah of Corals admitted to doing well out of Generous. "For six weeks before the race we were about the shortest price and the same was true on the day."

One well known big punter connected to the yard is believed to have had £7,000 on at 14–1, four times. Later that month he put £100,000 on Magic Ring at 2–1 at Royal Ascot. The two horses had earned him a cool £600,000. Word has it that a few owners, more out of loyalty to the yard than anything else, cleared £10,000.

Success also meant that Generous had become the first winner of the Derby to have gone through the sales ring since Secreto in 1984. Two others had cost more than his Ir 200,000 gns: Golden Fleece who cost $775,000 and Secreto himself who cost $340,000.

Plans were immediately launched to take Generous over to Ireland for the Irish Derby, the second leg of the High Summer Treble and what Anthony Penfold was later to describe as the 'New Triple Crown'. "Horses are there to be raced. If I cannot lose, I cannot win," said Prince Fahd describing his racing policy.

"When you have a horse like Generous, you don't make plans for them, they make them themselves. There was no argument, the Irish and then, all being well, the King George, was the obvious route," said the trainer.

The press squeezed into what must surely be the smallest room on the course for a post-race press conference. All members of the winning team answered questions. "Where next?" "We're not afraid of running him now, we'll take on anything, bring on Suave Dancer."

"When did you think you had it won?" And the inevitable, "How do you feel about Richard Quinn?" (Richard was riding at Beverley.) "Unfortunate," said Paul.

The press squirmed when Alan, a stranger to all this, answered questions. His single-minded approach to the job, his blunt refusal to discuss with them his retainer with Prince Fahd or what Keith Piggott had told him the night before or how he felt about Richard. A polite quote of what Keith Piggott had said would have made great copy. It put backs up; verging on the rude.

"If," says Alan whose greatest day was spoilt by the affair, "I could erase a part of my life it is that press conference after the Derby. I deserved what I got. It was a lesson learned and I'm a lot wiser for it now. I'd like to say some of the same things again but I never would. I thought at the time it was them being rude to me."

Prince Fahd, who said that he would watch the video 20 times that night pretending each time that he did not know the result, was invited to the Royal Box for tea. There, the Queen, remembering their meeting by the gate to the stands exclaimed: "You won it!"

"The whole thing was so wonderful especially after last year when Zoman was one of the favourites for the Derby," recalls Prince Fahd. "We went up to the Royal box then when Quest For Fame won. The Duke of Edinburgh had said to me: 'I thought you were going to win it with Zoman?' 'Yes,' I replied, 'but when I saw my father-in-law's horse coming we shouted to the jockey to stop.'

"There were so many clues to his winning the Derby," says Prince Fahd. "To be out of Doff The Derby who was by Master Derby. The trophy he won for the Reference Point Stakes was a sign-post pointing to Epsom."

Whatcombe moved to the Swan, Great Shefford for the evening and Derby day for the yard and all connected with it, the trainer included, ended in the small hours of Thursday morning.

Generous had returned home 12 kg lighter than he had set out that morning, a little more than the average horse loses in a mile and a half race and the same amount that he had lost in the Guineas.

But was it a great race? Either way Generous could have done no more than win as he did. The form of the others, well, Marju went on to win the Group 1 St James' Palace Stakes at Royal Ascot next time out, one of Europe's premier mile races although he had appeared to be staying on over Epsom's mile and a half. Star of Gdansk was third again in the Irish Derby and ran in some top mile races before winning the Group 3 Desmond Stakes over a mile in Ireland. Hector Protector went back to France and back to his winning ways for his next outing when he won the important Group 1 Prix Jacques Le Marois at Deauville in August, over a mile. Hundra spent the rest of the summer being campaigned abroad but he had saved his best for the Derby and was unplaced in three outings. Corrupt ran second to Zoman in the Scottish Classic and repaid Neville Callaghan's faith in him by winning the Group 2 Great

146

Voltigeur Stakes at York in August in tremendous style. Hokusai ran a creditable third to Marju in the St James's Palace. Hailsham ran a couple more times finishing behind Zoman and Corrupt in the Scottish Classic. Some of the biggest Derby disappointments went on to prove that pre-Derby confidence had not been misjudged. Toulon won at Maisons-Laffitte in July over an extended mile and a half before coming back to England to win the St Leger at Doncaster. Environment Friend went on to win the Group 1 Eclipse Stakes over a mile and a quarter and then ran second to Suave Dancer in the Irish Champion Stakes. Mystiko went on to prove there was another big race in him when he won the Group 2 Challenge Stakes over seven furlongs at Newmarket. But a mouthwatering clash between the French and English Derby winners awaited at the Curragh and it is to Ireland, just a few miles up the road from Barronstown Stud, where we must go next.

THE IRISH DERBY

The Budweiser Irish Derby on 30th June 1991 was always likely to be billed as a two horse race once it was confirmed that it was to be the objective of both Generous and Suave Dancer.

The latter had won the French Derby, the Prix du Jockey-Club, at Chantilly as equally impressively as Generous had won at Epsom. His greatest asset was clearly his blistering turn of foot at the end of a race. In many ways he was ideally suited to the typical 'French' style of racing, switched off out the back but with a devastating run waiting to be unleashed. At Chantilly he had beaten an average field in a slow run race in a matter of strides under Cash Asmussen for his young English but Chantilly based trainer John Hammond. But, like we said of Generous, he could do no more than win it emphatically.

History, though, was against him, no French trained horse had won both the French and Irish Derbys although Generous' sire Caerleon had achieved the feat trained from Ireland.

There was much to admire in both colts. Suave Dancer, a bay who had cost $45,000 as a yearling, was a day older than Generous. Both shared the same grandsire in Nijinsky, both had won on fast and soft ground, both had had the best part of a month to recover from their previous exertions and both were potential European Champions. This race, on neutral ground, was anticipated at the time, to be the decider.

Generous had continued to work well up on Woolley Down. Tommy Jennings had given him his final workout the Wednesday before although he had done nothing too searching at home since the Derby. Walter Swinburn had been over to France to sit on Suave Dancer; he was deputising for Cash Asmussen who had broken a collar bone riding in France. Paul Cole was bubbling with confidence. "Better than he was in the Derby," was his opinion. He had tightened security around Generous and Whatcombe, he wanted to take no chances. Lads took it in turn to sit outside the Derby winner's box. He also made the decision to fly Generous to The Curragh and back the same day from Southampton, remembering what had happened when Generous had stayed overnight in Deauville. Suave Dancer had arrived at the course on the Thursday evening prior to the Sunday race.

It may have been billed as a two horse race, perhaps a bit disappointing for the connections of the others, but there were in actual fact six who lined up for the contest worth £366,500 to the winner. Jim Bolger's Star of Gdansk was to renew rivalry with Generous, with this time, the aid of his own pacemaker Nordic Admirer. Vincent O'Brien was to run Sportsworld with Lester Piggott up. In a normal year it would have been inconceivable that the master of Ballydoyle was to run an unbeaten horse, three out of three as a three-year-old, and for it to be virtually ignored in the betting. The other runner was opportunist permit-holder Luke Comer's Barry's Run, still a maiden after 19 starts, who was guaranteed the valuable £12,000 on offer to the sixth placed horse providing he completed the course.

A modern day record crowd of 28,000 arrived at The Curragh for the clash. The atmosphere was electric. "If," says Prince Fahd, "the Epsom Derby was my greatest moment, then running Generous in the Irish Derby was my most challenging. It was a very scary race to watch."

The race lived up to hype. In the Derby and, later in the King George, Alan Munro could have afforded to make tactical errors so great were the winning margins but in Ireland he was forced to make a decision early in the race. Barry's Run and pacemaker Nordic Admirer made the early running but the pace was not fast enough for Generous who was fighting Alan for his head. If he tried to hold him in behind he was going to play into Suave Dancer's hands and yet he would be taking a certain risk by letting Generous pass the leaders and do his own dirty work. He decided on the second of the two options and let Generous bowl his way into the lead despite there being over a mile and a furlong of the wide open Curragh remaining.

"He was fighting me, he likes to use himself in a race and doesn't like to dawdle," recalls Alan. "For me as a rider it was very uncomfortable in behind. I really had little choice but to let him go and once he got to the front he settled immediately."

Suave Dancer made progress from the back about five furlongs out ready to make his challenge. Star of Gdansk was already being ridden along and an almighty roar went up from the stands as Sportsworld moved into second as they turned into the straight. In front Alan had quickened the pace again and at the two furlong pole the two horse race that had been predicted was becoming a reality. Sportsworld dropped away, Star of Gdansk was making no impression. It was between the two Derby winners, Generous in front, Suave Dancer the challenger.

Two furlongs to race and the French horse's challenge looked ominous, we were expecting that devastating turn of foot. At the furlong pole Suave Dancer still had a chance. "I saw him looming up on me," says Alan. "I feared it was all over. But Generous put his ears back, I could feel him dig himself out, he did not want to get beat." Even if Swinburn had thought it was just a question of picking Generous off, Suave Dancer never got closer than three quarters of a length off Generous. Inside that final furlong the son of Caerleon reasserted himself over the French colt to win by three lengths.

It had indeed been a clash of the titans. Star of Gdansk was eight lengths further away in third, two lengths in front of Sportsworld. Nordic Admirer followed him home at a respectful distance and Barry's Run did indeed collect his £12,000 for completing.

"It was a better performance than when he won the Epsom Derby," says Alan. "He had to go out there by himself for a mile and make the pace because he wouldn't settle. I think he would have been more impressive on better ground."

Walter Swinburn riding Suave Dancer also thought the ground against his horse but predicted he would make a terrific four-year-old.

Generous had become the 11th horse to complete the English–Irish Derby double. Paul Cole was immediately keen to take on the older horses, including possibly his stablemate Snurge, in the King George. The trainer was full of praise for his jockey who had, he said, ridden the perfect race. "We were afraid the others would want to slow it down to try and beat us and when there was no pace, he had the intelligence to go on." John Hammond, trainer of the runner up, summed up the feelings of all who had attended the Irish Derby. "It was a great race," he said. "Generous won on merit and full credit to him. Suave Dancer will be stronger later in the year but make no mistake, he was beaten here by a very, very good horse."

"But," he added significantly, "I'm looking forward to taking him on in the Arc." Prince Fahd was just as keen. "That," he said "is what racing is all about."

After the race Henri Chaloub Suave Dancer's owner came over to congratulate Prince Fahd. This, too, is what racing is all about.

THE KING GEORGE

The timing of the King George VI and Queen Elizabeth Diamond Stakes is ideal for a horse that has run in both the English and Irish Derbys. It comes a month after the Curragh.

If there were any doubters of Generous' ability before Saturday 27th July then there can surely have been none after Prince Fahd's colt had joined the exclusive club of 'High Summer Treble' winners, Nijinsky, The Minstrel, Troy and Shergar. As his price 4–6 suggested (second favourite Saddler's Hall was 6–1) few anticipated defeat. And nor could they could have anticipated the emphatic style in which Generous was to annihilate his elders whom he was meeting for the first time. Selecting a runner-up was to prove an infinitely harder task for punters.

Paul Cole was nervous beforehand though. He did not show it, outwardly cool and collected. Generous had come out of the Irish Derby very well but had put on weight and, no matter what exercise Paul had given the colt, he was unable to shift it. He had been unable to tell if Generous had come on for his race in Ireland but could only think he was as well as he had been there.

But in the race, run on a gloriously warm July afternoon, Generous was up against some respected older horses. The 1990 French Derby winner Sanglamore had again won at Chantilly the same day as Suave Dancer and followed it up by finishing third in the Eclipse at Sandown. Rock Hopper had already had a busy summer; Michael Stoute was putting blinkers on him for the first

152

time. He had won the Group 2 Princess of Wales' Stakes at Newmarket and prior to that had run second in the Group 1 Grand Prix de Saint-Cloud. At Royal Ascot he had won the Group 2 Hardwicke Stakes. Sapience had been behind Rock Hopper at Newmarket and as such represented little threat. Clive Brittain's grey Terimon was one capable of pulling off a shock. He had finished second to Nashwan in the 1989 Derby at odds of 500–1.

The four-year-old filly Tiger Flower was lightly raced and, despite representing Sheikh Mohammed and Henry Cecil, the combination responsible for the 1990 King George first and second, Belmez and Old Vic, her Listed race second was clearly not good enough. It was doubtful whether she had the experience for such a race.

Among the three-year-olds was Generous' old rival Hailsham who he had met in the Derby. Clive Brittain, his and Terimon's trainer, was also fielding Luchiroverte, the French Derby fourth although he was still a maiden at the time. He had subsequently won the Churchill Stakes at Ascot on Heath Day but he looked entered in hope rather than confidence.

Finally, last but not least, there was Michael Stoute's other runner Saddler's Hall, Generous' nearest market rival. He had shown marked improvement last time out to win the Group 2 King Edward VII Stakes at Royal Ascot. He had, under Lester Piggott, made all the running and had won as he liked. The great man was in the saddle again on the 27th.

Perhaps more significant from the racing purist's point of view at the time were those intended runners who had, for one reason or another, failed to make it: Stagecraft who had been second in the Eclipse; Epervier Bleu whose departure took the international flavour out of the contest; In The Groove and Generous' stable companion Snurge.

Apart from the extra poundage Generous was carrying, Paul Cole, outwardly confident about the race, was

153

worried about the tactics Alan Munro should employ. He did not want Alan getting hemmed in on the rail behind a tiring pacemaker so he made him watch numerous videos of previous King Georges. Under no circumstances was he to be stuck on the rail around the last bend.

The race was off on time, 3.20, and run at a blistering pace. Ray Cochrane, acting to Clive Brittain's orders set off like a scalded cat on Hailsham. Lester tracked him, at a respectable distance, on Saddler's Hall. Luchiroverte and Frankie Dettori sat third with Generous, avoiding the inside back in fourth. The pace was blistering and before the turn for home, when that famous bell rings, Lester had already taken it up, Generous had moved smoothly through into second and Hailsham had proved he was not up to sprinting further than seven furlongs. Behind him Sanglamore, at one stage 20 lengths off the leader, was moving up from the rear, Rock Hopper had moved into fourth, Tiger Flower and Terimon were further back.

Lester was up to his old tricks when he hit the front, slowing the pace down going into the bend he hoped he might concertina the field then slip it coming off into the straight. Generous was looming through, just waiting to be allowed to go.

Alan unleashed him just over two furlongs out. The effect was devastating. In a matter of strides he had left the rest for dead. A furlong out and, after their initial silence, the silence of surprise, the crowd started applauding their appreciation. They were witnessing a real champion in action.

Alan, crouching in his instantly recognisable style, whip pointing to the sky, was able to ease down and glance through his legs to see where the opposition had gone.

The official winning distance was seven lengths. It was a record for the race. Mill Reef and Dahlia had won by six lengths but no horse had treated his opposition with quite so much disdain as Generous. Sanglamore had finished second. Rock Hopper was a length away in third and Terimon another length and a half back in fourth.

Pat Eddery who had ridden Sanglamore was moved to say: "Generous was fantastic. He really quickened over the last two furlongs and that must put him in the same league as Dancing Brave. Without him in the race Sanglamore would have been a decent winner."

Compliments did not come from Eddery alone although if he put him in the Dancing Brave mould, who are we to argue? Men with experience of brilliant horses were equally impressed. Steve Cauthen, who rode Tiger Flower said he had never seen a horse take off like Generous had after such a fast run race. Bruce Raymond, with 25 years of raceriding experience behind him put it more simply: "The best I have ever seen."

Comparisons with the greats, Mill Reef and Nijinsky were now perfectly acceptable. Before you did not dare mention the name Generous in the same breath as the recognised all-time greats. For many there that day it was the most electrifying performance they had ever witnessed. Generous, had proved in the two Derbys that he could grind his opposition into submission with his gallop and stamina, here he had not only outstayed his opposition he had quickened clear of it and shown a champion's turn of foot.

For Alan the fairytale summer had continued. "I had ridden Generous twice before the King George and thought I knew what he was capable of. I didn't think any horse could quicken after the gallop we had done. I thought he would just stay on. It was really awesome and frightened the life out of me."

For BBC Radio 5 Luca Cumani, the Newmarket trainer, could not contain his excitement. He had just seen what he considered a true champion in action. "I feel sorry for anyone not able to make it to Ascot today," he said. "They have missed out."

155

Prince Fahd was one of those, he had been unable to make it for the King George. "I was at home watching it live through Dubai Television. I just couldn't believe the electrifying performance that he gave. It was unbelievable to see Alan ease up like he did and still win so far. I'm glad I was able to see it live on T.V. The thing I missed most about not being there was meeting the Queen."

But there was a sad note to the day, as it was made clear following this great victory that Generous was likely to have only one more race, the Arc, after which he would be retired to stud.

Recently the few Derby winners which have stayed in training at four have not trained on. Prince Fahd had to look no further than his father-in-law's Quest For Fame and Sanglamore to see this. "It is seen as being very sporting but most end up regretting it," says Anthony Penfold.

"Prince Fahd needs to capitalise on Generous though. He owns 65 horses which is a lot of employment for a lot of people. Indirectly every time he is an underbidder on a horse at the sales (20 a year) he is benefiting stud staff. If there had been no Generous in 1991 there was every chance Prince Fahd would be considering a cut-back on his racing operation. If we had had another 1989 he couldn't justify the high level of investment. If Generous did not happen to train on his value could drop by a third and if he does he is not going to add to his value in a falling market."

Paul Cole was equally philosophical about it. "Of course I'd love to train him as a four-year-old but Prince Fahd needs a success like this to go on investing in racing. He has borrowed money to finance the operation and that, as we all know, is an expensive job. He has done it in the hope that one day a horse would come along that would enable him to re-finance the whole operation. Now, it goes without saying that when Generous, the horse that gave him the wherewithal to do it, came along he had

156

no alternative but to capitalise. It is a fact of life."

Prince Fahd was sorry that he had to cash in on Generous when he did. "I really wish I could keep him running as a four-year-old but for financial reasons it is impossible," he says. "When I was asked about it I said 'If someone comes up with £5 million for doing so I would be able to do it'. One of these days I might have another one like him and we might be able to afford to keep in training as a four-year-old."

Nevertheless the pros and cons of his retirement kept the letters pages of both *The Racing Post* and *The Sporting Life* busy for weeks afterwards.

Details of his syndication were released a month after Ascot. It was already known that he would be standing at Prince Fahd's father-in-law's (Khalid Abdullah) Banstead Manor Stud at Cheveley, near Newmarket. There he would be joining Rainbow Quest and Warning. His paper value was set at around £8 million. The 45 shares in Generous were being offered at £175,000 each.

Generous' valuation demonstrated the recent drop in market values for bloodstock. The 1979 Derby winner Troy was syndicated for £7.2 m, allowing for inflation, considerably more than Generous. His value was put at just over half that of Dancing Brave who was syndicated for £14m after he had won the Arc. Had Prince Fahd been open to offers from Japan and from Ireland where Coolmore was keen to have Generous back to stand with Caerleon at his birthplace, then Prince Fahd would have raised more. But as they said at Coolmore after a higher offer had been rejected: "Blood is thicker than money."

Arc Diary: Monday, 30th September, 1991

IT has been a fruitful year all round at Whatcombe. Despite the weather the weekend wasn't too bad either. Culture Vulture substantially added to the coffers on Saturday, putting Paul Cole over £400,000 ahead of his nearest rival in the trainers' championship.

It rained across Europe but Generous handled the soft, as well as he does the good, in a Saturday workout at Newbury. And Snurge, the stable's other Arc contender? Well, his chances are enhanced by every drop that falls on Longchamp. Maybe Richard Quinn will have the last laugh after all, though Generous' supporters in the camp won't hear of it.

The last time we were here in early June the elders were in flower, brambles and elegant dogroses raged rampantly over Whatcombe's downland hedgerows. Autumn's here now; the change in the weather, the darker mornings, the presence of blackberries, rose-hips and crab apples signify the end of another fruitful season. This week, Cole hopes, will be as fruitful as the rest of the summer.

Generous is no stranger to big-race preparation now. This far down the road even an unintelligent horse would have twigged that he is going through the last throes of that familiar routine which culminates in a race. Two racecourse gallops on consecutive weekends, the constant attention. How wonderfully fit he must feel.

Despite running in the 2,000 Guineas back in May, he should be fresh. He had a three-week break after the King George. Cole has always emphasised the difficulty of getting an English three-year-old to October feeling as well as his French counterparts, who have been trained with this race in mind all season. The French horses are like confident high-jumpers coming into the competition when the bar is high. Generous is the high-jumper who has cleared every round.

158

Monday. There's a lot for the trainer to organise and delegate. He's got to put the finishing touches on Generous and Snurge. He's got a hundred others to train besides. He wants to be in Newmarket to buy the next Generous at the Highflyer Sales and he wants a good look at what's on offer first. He would normally stay up there, this week he will commute.

There's the nightmare scenario, Generous' intended flight to France being fog-bound on Sunday morning. Could he fly out of RAF Lyneham instead of Southampton? It's on top of a hill, theoretically less chance of fog. Who knows the base commander? Ironically Snurge is claustrophobic and, short of hiring a jumbo, is better off going by boat. Plans, like the weather forecast, have a degree of fluidity about them.

Out in the yard two camera crews jostle in gentlemanly fashion for the best shots. "Don't stand there, you'll frighten the horses," says Colin Ratcliffe, the head lad.

"Which is Generous?" they ask.

They want to interview the trainer and horseracing plainly isn't a specialist subject for some of them, but they find Cole genial. He politely rephrases a daft question for them before answering it.

You begin to feel you know why human superstars can't always cope with the constant bother but Generous, looking immaculate, really isn't worried. The fuss might just as well be about another horse.

He and Snurge are set apart from the rest of the string on this cold, sunny but crisp morning. They wear smart striped Witney exercise blankets, the others are clothed in their lighter, blue sheets.

Tommy Jennings, the work-rider, gives Generous two canters up the all-weather, one routine, one sharp. In contrast to Derby week he is no longer turned out in a cage after first lot. It's colder and he's more valuable, considerably so, and the risk of injury at this stage outweighs the benefits of a buck and a kick. But the armful of handpicked grass, devotedly harvested by Jennings, that's the same.

Arc Diary: Tuesday, 1st October, 1991

SEVEN o'clock on a damp morning. Whatcombe lads pull on their waterproofs, some put hoods on their horses in preparation for a wet first lot.

First light and we are not greeted by birdsong. Instead a 'muck' lorry, with its long hydraulic arm, its engine straining, groans and creaks as it grabs another mouthful of steaming straw from the muckheap. The mushrooms you had for breakfast are grown in this stuff.

Tommy Jennings has tacked up Generous. He puts the finishing touches to the colt, wipes his eyes and nostrils with a sponge dipped in disinfectant. Like a child having chocolate removed from his face, Generous shakes his head, tries to avoid it. "I know you don't like it," reassures Jennings reaching up.

Paul Cole, in sales attire, directs Jennings. He and a lead horse, Ambassador Royale, are off to Woolley for a canter. The lead is really only there for company.

The weather takes a turn for the better. Generous' hood is unnecessary now and so are waterproofs. The two horses walk and trot to the gallop, are directed across the busy Wantage — Hungerford road by Doug Prior, the gallopman. His first job in the morning is to stop the traffic. He knows Woolley Down better than anyone, having tended it when Arthur Budgett trained at Whatcombe.

"I've never seen any mud up here except in the gateway," says Jennings. The ground after weekend rain on the never-ploughed turf is perfect. The two horses have the 100 acres to themselves. Not even the trainer is there — he's gone to Newbury to see Snurge work on his way to Newmarket.

You would assume there was a lot of pressure on Jennings. He's riding £7.75 million worth of horseflesh, ironically in a pair of old-fashioned rubber wellingtons with the tops turned over because the soles have fallen off his jodhpur boots. It's some contrast. You'd think he was under the same sort of pressure as a Ryder Cup golfer on the Ocean Course. He need only tread on the wrong stone—there are plenty of flints around—and the subsequent bruising could rule Generous out of the Arc. His work-rider is much like the horse in that respect, not bothered by it all.

"It's very hard to say if he's improved since the Derby," he says on the way home. "You'd have some people tell you a horse has improved 10lb but you can't put a figure on it. I can definitely tell you he's not deteriorated though, that's easier to gauge.

"He's the only horse I've ever ridden that never whipped round or bucked. He stood up on his hind legs on Woolley just before the Irish Derby when he was upset by some horses working past him, that's all. People ask if he's any different to ride from other horses but he's not. It's only his ability that sets him apart. Take a horse like Ibn Bey, he was different. Always spinning round, backwards, you'd be hanging off him half the time, he was difficult."

Generous can be strong, Jennings confirms. "When he worked in front of the crowd at Newbury ten days ago, he was keen. He's not like some horses that say 'I'm going to cart you whatever you do' but he can be a bit wooden-mouthed. That day I was having a job to hold him behind Monarda and I was glad to let him go a furlong out.

"Last Saturday it was a different story. He settled beautifully. But," he confides changing the subject, "that whip of Alan Munro's is pretty awesome. Five furlongs out last Saturday I got to him very easily and he was having to push Monarda to go fast enough for us. He got his whip out and started turning it through his fingers. I thought I was overtaking a hedgetrimmer—I don't think a timid horse would want to pass him, you know!"

Back at home Jennings brushes the sweaty girth and

saddle marks from Generous; within minutes you wouldn't know he'd been out. Robert Latham won't find any sweat on him at evening stables, that's for sure. Assistant trainer Rupert Arnold dabs cod liver oil on his heels, a precaution to stop them cracking. It is always a worry with white pasterns like Generous'. Jennings picks out mud from his hind feet at the same time, and when they are up blacksmith Alfie Hall makes a brief inspection.

He'll plate him in front on Friday, behind on Saturday. "Just to give the front ones time to settle down a bit," he explains.

In the office the phone rings. The boss is checking that all is well. Another day closer, Generous is a chip shot from the flag. There are a couple of bunkers between him and the green but, one hopes, no alligators lurking in the rough.

Arc Diary: Wednesday, 2nd October, 1991

WEDNESDAY at Whatcombe, always a busy day. An apprentice hurriedly tacks up horses for jockeys Richard Quinn, Alan Munro and Chris Rutter. They waltz in, distinguished in felt-covered riding hats instead of crash helmets, a couple of minutes before Colin Ratcliffe gives the OK for everyone to pull out. How the apprentice wishes he could be a jockey.

Generous and Tommy Jennings hold another press conference. First lot every day is a press conference now. Two camera crews, a photographer, a journalist or two. Give Cole credit for being so open, what he's doing is so good for the sport. And for the first time you begin to get the impression that Generous is beginning to like all the attention too. Before he was unmoved by it, now there's just a twinkle in his eye. It suggests he knows that he is the big attraction.

It is his last morning for a semi-serious piece of work. A mile and a furlong to be led by Monarda, again. "Let him settle," says Cole from his hack at the collecting ring above Woolley Down to Jennings. "Then let him enjoy himself."

You have to feel sorry for Monarda. He must be the most pissed-off horse in training. "I think he's had enough of it now," reflects Cole about Generous' lead horse. As he must by now be resigned, he makes the running and is joined three furlongs from the end by Generous, who then proceeds to leave him, apparently standing still.

Anthony Penfold, Fahd Salman's racing manager, has a suitable epithet for Monarda, though. His services have not gone unnoticed and will get a mention in despatches. "He's done us well, you don't often get a lead horse like this who wins three races in a season and he's led others apart from Generous." Give him his due, it has taken the home-bred, a half-brother to Magic Ring, until October to get browned off with his job. But it must be a bit like me giving Seb Coe a lead. I'd pretty soon want to give up athletics.

In the kitchen there is kedgeree, Canadian honey and confidence on the breakfast table. In the yard there's tension but there's a confidence in here that wasn't so evident before the Derby.

Racing photos on the back wall fight for room like a maximum field round Chester. The lion's share are now of Generous, there's Ibn Bey in the Irish St Leger, Beeshi in the Foy, Reach in the Royal Lodge, Snurge in the Leger, Ruby Tiger in the E P Taylor, John de Coombe in the Salamandre, the photo-finish when Insan got beat a whisker in the Irish Derby, and more. It is a pictorial history of Whatcombe's last 15 years.

"It will take a true Group I horse to beat him provided he's a hundred per cent," says Cole. "There's only really one other in the race and that's Suave Dancer. I think the rest can only be hopeful.

"There's always a temptation to overdo a horse before a big race," he adds, referring to the gallop he had just given Generous. "Nobody could be more pleased with the horse. He's fit, his weight is right (497kg last Sunday) and there is no doubt he's in good form, he's running away with his work partners. He must be feeling good."

Psychologically he has Generous spot-on. The horse did not just want to pass Monarda in that gallop, get a head in front and call it a day. No way, he wanted to annihilate Monarda, go all the way to the top and this is just a regular gallop at home. How will he feel when he's wound up a bit in Paris on Sunday? He doesn't just want to win the gallop, he wants to win by as far as possible. It is the attitude of a champion.

"We won't know precisely how right he is until after the race, you never do," announces Cole in between mouthfuls of fish and rice. "We know he's firing though, we're not going there like you do with some horses before a big race, taking the chance and hoping they're firing. We know he is."

Cole is happy now about his decision to fly Generous to France on Saturday instead of Sunday morning. "If you've got two horses of the same ability," he says "and one has had a four-hour trip that morning, then the local horse will, all things being equal, win." He doesn't want to give Suave Dancer that sort of advantage.

Vincent O'Brien offered his advice to Cole on the subject at the sales on Tuesday. It helped him make his mind up. "He said there was no choice," recalled Cole. "If we go on the day we risk the weather, turbulence, a hold-up with the plane, customs. I'll be much happier if he gets there on Saturday.

"And it will give me the perfect excuse if he gets beat," he adds with a grin. About Cole's own travel plans? "Myself?" he asks. "I think I'll go to Butlins for the weekend."

Arc Diary: Thursday, 3rd October, 1991

GENEROUS, in a light drizzle, canters once quietly up the all-weather. Six furlongs on the collar. At this stage in his preparation, it is no more than you or I walking down to the shops—just a stretch. Tommy Jennings reports him as fine, no problems.

Assistant Rupert Arnold and head lad Colin Ratcliffe (Paul Cole is away) are visibly relieved. They don't want to see him tread on a stone now. Memories of Belmez, who flew to Paris last year with his foot in a bucket of ice. Just how would you begin to break that sort of news to your boss? So by 8am it is, to all intents and purposes, another day over as far as Generous, tucked up safe and sound back in his box, is concerned.

Meanwhile the circus that is the Flat racing industry has camped down in Newmarket, until it gets its passports out at the weekend. Not for nothing is it known as 'Headquarters'. Four days of high-class racing, three nights of valuable yearling sales.

There are people here, people not directly involved, to whom Generous winning the Arc will mean so much. Like the former stable lad who got out of racing six months ago. He is aching, like an addict going 'cold turkey', to get back into racing. It depends entirely on a bet he's struck on Generous. It will make or break him financially. It is unlikely to cure him of horses.

David Nagle, breeder of Generous, owner of Barronstown Stud, is just another of the characters standing at the back of the busy, smoky, Tatts sales ring. Everyone has a favourite place to stand and this is his, hardly visible.

A former Goffs auctioneer himself, he was selling four lots last night but was interested in a yearling out of a mare he'd sold some time back. His mind is firmly on the evening's business. They may lead good lives, some of them, but these stud owners have to sweat, like jockeys in a sauna, between now and December. The profit or loss on two years' work will be decided in a couple of minutes inside this ring.

At the back of his mind is Sunday. He has Generous' dam, Doff The Derby, and a half-brother foal by Last Tycoon who is at Coolmore Stud at the moment. This sales ring, Nagle anticipates, will be the venue for that colt's first public appearance. He is likely to be entered for the December Foal Sales here. It will be a guaranteed crowd-puller and he looks the part.

"It would be very arrogant to think it can happen again," confides Nagle, referring to Sunday. "He is already one of the great horses. People tell me he is better than Nijinsky over a mile and a half. You know, I never thought I'd look over the box door of a horse that was good enough to be mentioned in the same sentence."

Nagle was at Epsom (a gateman refused him entry to the winner's enclosure), The Curragh and Ascot. "We used to own a share in Attitude Adjuster. We're jumping folk at heart. I had tears in my eyes when he won at Cheltenham and I never thought I'd be moved to tears by a Flat horse, but when the crowd started clapping a furlong out in the King George, I was having trouble holding them back. They only do that for real athletes. I wouldn't miss the Arc for anything."

Generous is unique among recent Derby winners. He was not only on offer to the world's best judges of horseflesh once, but twice. He was pinhooked as a foal by Hamish Alexander, who bought him for Ir80,000gns and sold him on at Goffs Cartier Million Sales 11 months later for Ir200,000gns. It looked a good deal at the time!

Alexander owns Partridge Close Stud in Durham. He has two yearlings to sell at these sales, people to meet, people to speak to, agents to whom he must show off his produce. He's running around like a blue-arsed fly—catch him if you can.

On Saturday, when half the characters at this sale will up sticks and head for Paris, he'll be on his way to Goffs in Ireland with two more yearlings to sell. On Sunday he'll watch the Arc on television.

He watched the Derby on television after a morning's fishing on the Spey; he listened to the King George on the car radio and "nearly took out three buses". The only time he saw Generous run in the flesh was in the Prix Morny, when he finished last. "I don't think it would be very fair on the horse if I were to go to France," he says superstitiously. "It was wonderful listening to the King George; I was riding a finish at the driving wheel. The children thought I'd finally gone potty."

You get the full spectrum at the sales. Helping out Alexander is Malcolm Rippon, a former lad turned betting shop assistant. He'd make good biography material, far more interesting than many of the 'famous' whose life stories make it to print.

A brief curriculum vitae. Rippon was apprenticed to Sir Jack Jarvis, worked for Sir Noel Murless, looked after Busaca, a very good filly, for Peter Walwyn, played football for Peterborough United and was held at gunpoint in his betting shop on last Cheltenham Gold Cup day while two hoods cleaned out the till. He led up the yearling Generous for Alexander at Goffs. He's always been lucky with horses. Peter Walwyn pointed the fact out to Alexander at Goffs.

He sits outside Partridge Close's allotted boxes in Somerville Paddock. He holds the very bridle with which he led the yearling Generous. The National Horseracing Museum might be asking for it after Sunday. "I think the best race he ran was in the Irish Derby. They tried to run the race to get him beat. And for a horse to pull like he did and then go again, I didn't believe it was possible."

Beside him stands the little girl who once brushed out that famous flaxen tail. She just might have people wanting her autograph on Sunday night!

Arc Diary: Friday, 4th October, 1991

FOUR horses set out for a mist shrouded Woolley Down. Generous, Ambassador Royale, Retouch and the hack. We talked of the quiet before the storm prior to the Derby. We're here again, only the Arc rates higher on the Beaufort Scale. Let no-one underestimate this race.

Normally first-lot talk is of last night's television viewing and sex, in either order. It usually gets a bit more sophisticated through second lot but, predictably, chat between the four this morning is of the race.

"He's a great horse whether he wins or gets beat," says Colin Ratcliffe, on the hack. "None of those other great horses who won the Derby and King George went to Ireland in between," adds Tommy Jennings.

Generous, three lengths behind Ambassador Royale, canters routinely towards the top of Woolley. Possibly, sadly, it will be for the last time in his short career. Halfway up they emerge, like two spitfires above the clouds, from the mist that veils the valley in which the gallop begins.

Everyone is relaxed. Four horses, four riders. The view is of Fawley church atop the opposite hill, its spire spotlighted by the rising sun. Not a soul in sight. What a contrast to Longchamp. They want to keep Generous relaxed like this for as long as possible now.

He wasn't bothered when his neighbour Zoman left Whatcombe at 2.30am to catch the 6.30am sailing from Dover with Snurge.

He'll have a normal canter during first lot tomorrow. "He's intelligent," says Jennings. "If you just took him for a lead out he'd know something was up."

He'll leave Whatcombe for his flight to France mid-afternoon, with Culture Vulture and Magic Ring. Their arrival will be precision-timed. The Longchamp stables are cleaned out after racing between 6.30pm and 7.30pm. They don't want to hang around waiting for a box.

With them on the plane will be assistant Rupert Arnold and Cole's vet, James Maine. He'll be the next most important person on the flight after the pilot. Hopefully, he won't be needed.

Generous' lad Robert Latham has been looking forward to this trip since the King George. He's enjoyed waiting for this.

"He's just as well, if not better, than he was in the King George. I don't think the night away will upset him. I'd be more worried about the pre-race parade."

Latham's anticipation is tinged with a certain sadness. "He's been a good bread-earner for me," admits Latham, but looking after Generous has meant more to him than just being a few quid better off. Remember, looking after a champion like this is the ultimate for a lad.

"Horses like this only come in ones, for trainers and for us lads alike. I want him to do it so badly because it would make him one of the greatest horses of all time."

But even if this is their last trip to the races together, all is not lost for Latham. When Generous trots out of the yard for the last time, on to the 69 bus for Banstead Manor, into his place will step a yearling Lomond colt, his half-brother, already assigned to Latham.

But of Sunday, Latham stresses: "I so want him to win." And you know he wants victory so badly, desperately, not for his sake, not for Cole's sake, not for Fahd Salman's sake, but for Generous' sake. Don't we all?

THE ARC

The Prix de L'Arc de Triomphe has proved a graveyard for some of Britain's greatest racehorses in the past. Paul Cole was fully aware of that fact. Generous had been in hard training for a long time and, whereas Suave Dancer had been given a holiday following the Irish Derby, Generous had been kept on the go for another month for the King George.

The plan had always been to go straight from the King George to the Arc without a prep-race. Paul believed that many horses lost their Arcs and reputations in these lesser group races when they were not fully wound up.

Nevertheless Generous, who had been installed as the 4–5 favourite for the Arc within seconds of his crossing the line at Ascot, was to have a holiday, turned out in the cage pens at Whatcombe, taking it easy, before his Arc build-up.

His work was stepped up towards the end of August and through early September. On Saturday 21st September, a fortnight before the Arc, he was taken to Newbury for a racecourse gallop. It was a decent day's racing with the Mill Reef Stakes and the Autumn Cup but there was a big turn out to witness the public workout run as a 'first race'. It was a big draw, Generous' last appearance on a British racecourse and what a performance he turned in. It was quite frankly the most impressive workout I have ever seen, what power he showed when Tommy Jennings let him go. If that was not the Generous of Epsom, The Curragh and Ascot, then what was? And everyone present agreed.

The Arc was 'supposed' to be Generous' glorious swansong. Excepting physical ill-being what could beat him? Suave Dancer was the big French hope, stronger than he had been mid-summer, well handled by John Hammond, Cash Asmussen back in the plate and full of confidence. He had since won the Irish Champion Stakes over a mile and a quarter. The race was billed Generous versus Suave Dancer, the Re-match.

This time though it was Generous who was up against history. No horse had won 'The High Summer Treble' and the Arc. The draw had not been kind either. In the Derby he had been drawn 10 and he was the fifth winner to emerge from that stall in the last six years at Epsom. Here he was drawn 14 of 14 and the French are particular about crossing over to the rails during the early stage of a race. But there were other problems.

"It is not easy to get a three-year-old through a Classic campaign and get him to Longchamp firing on all six cylinders," said Paul beforehand although he still exuded confidence.

The Arc has historically been a peculiar race; it throws up some surprise results from time to time and few of the fourteen runners could be ignored.

Apart from the market leaders, Generous and Suave Dancer, who were stirring up patriotic support much like a rugger international between England and France would, there were others. Paul Cole also saddled stable companion Snurge who had been third last year. He was unbeaten in three outings this year but, although he had won, he had never been that impressive. Roger Charlton ran the 1990 Derby winner Quest For Fame, still searching for his first win of the season. David Elsworth was bullish about In The Groove's chances; the Arc is a good race for fillies. Luca Cumani also ran a filly in Shamshir. She had failed to win as a three-year-old but had run well and been Group placed through the summer.

Ireland was represented by Jim Bolger's Jet Ski Lady, winner of the Oaks, America by the seven-year-old El Senor, winner of 12 of his 40 races. The home team, captained by Suave Dancer as it were, was strong. Group 3 winner Art Bleu, a four-year-old, was to pacemake for the younger Pistolet Bleu who had been layed out for the race and the four-year-old filly Miss Alleged. Of the other three-year-olds St Leger winner Toulon looked good for Andre Fabre and Pat Eddery. Pigeon Voyageur had won a Group 1 in Italy last time out, and last but not least the cheap-bred consistent filly Magic Night. Her trainer Philippe Dermercastel had only taken her because no one else wanted her. Her rise to the top was already the stuff of fairytales; could she really pull off the big one for her connections?

The day began well for Whatcombe. Culture Vulture, an immensely tough two-year-old filly followed her victory eight days before in the Brent Walker Fillies' Mile at Ascot by winning the Prix Marcel Boussac in a thrilling finish. British runners were having a field day. Keen Hunter won the Prix de L'Abbaye. Magic Ring, another two-year-old, ran a heroic race to finish third to give Whatcombe its second confidence booster of the afternoon. The scene was set.

Thousands of British people (10,000 was the estimate) thronged the enclosures and paddock. It was more like a day at Ascot, you'd have hardly guessed you were in France. The excitement was fever pitch. Paul Cole remained calm and confident. Generous remained calm in the paddock and through the parade.

The pacemaker Art Bleu did his job well in the race ensuring a strong pace, too fast according to Cash Asmussen who was biding his time in the rear with Suave Dancer. He led until they had fanned out into Long-champ's wide straight. Behind him Alan Munro was prominent on Generous towards the outside. The attention of British racegoers' binoculars were focused on Generous' famous green colours. He was perfectly poised. Suave Dancer, worth a glance, appeared to be too far out of his ground. And then the unbelievable, three furlongs out and Generous had gone from cruising to struggling, Alan sent out the distress signals. At Ascot he had won in a matter of strides, here in France he had been beaten in less. The British crowd sighed in disappointment and disbelief. At the same time Cash Asmussen had moved Suave Dancer up from the back along the outside; he was still waiting to unleash his run. Here it came, a furlong when he passed his rivals and left them standing. Too soon thought his trainer John Hammond and although he hung right and made hard work of that last half a furlong he had put a winning distance between him and the running-on Magic Night. It was Suave Dancer's day and the French loved it. In reality we all did, the turn of foot that left good horses standing in a fashion not witnessed at Longchamp since Dancing Brave. The same qualities that had endeared Generous to the racing public at Ascot in the King George were now endearing Suave Dancer to Paris.

Magic Night was two lengths second, Pistolet Bleu another length away in third. Toulon had run well in fourth, Pigeon Voyageur had got into trouble in the straight and it had cost him a place. The French had trained the first five home. Then came In The Groove, Quest For Fame followed by Generous, El Senor who had been slow away from the stalls, Shamshir, Miss Alleged, the pacemaker Art Bleu, Jet Ski Lady and last of all Snurge who had hit his head on the stalls.

The distance between Suave Dancer and Generous was nine lengths. He had finished too far down the field for it to be true. It was a disappointing end to a glittering career. And while the French crowds cheered the triumphant Suave Dancer and Cash, his helmet raised aloft in salute, they booed Generous. It was not deserved.

"The Arc was a sad day for me and for the horse," recalls Alan Munro of his last ride on Generous. "It is best forgotten. Right up to the last three furlongs he was going as well as ever and when I needed the burst he fell in a hole. It was ironic really because it was the first time I had expected the acceleration but I didn't get it.

"All I can say is that he wasn't there. Many people said I went too fast, it may be a valid criticism, but the third horse was in front of me all the way and perhaps those people don't realise how fast we went at Ascot. If I had gone slower we may have come in marginally closer but we would never have won. He seemed more relaxed at Longchamp. Perhaps that was a bad sign. It is a great pity because the Arc is the race they will all judge him on in years to come."

"And the booing?" I asked. "I think they were booing me not the horse," says Alan. "You don't blame the horse on those occasions."

Afterwards Prince Fahd, as dignified in defeat as in victory, remembered The Curragh when Henri Chalboub had congratulated him on victory. Prince Fahd went up to Chalboub, from the Lebanon, and gave him an Arabian hug. "I knew exactly how he felt after the Irish Derby," recalls Prince Fahd. "I was very pleased for him."

The Arc was a big disappointment for Prince Fahd. "If he had been second, third or even fourth, you could have said he was beaten by a better horse but to be beaten so far there must have been something wrong somewhere. Although take nothing away from Suave Dancer, it was a privilege to run with him in Ireland."

Back at home a blood test revealed a high fibrinogen level, 25 per cent higher than it was when he had a blood test taken half way through his two-year-old season. "Unless you are taking blood tests once a week which they don't do at Whatcombe it is hard to evaluate a one-off

176

test," says vet James Maine. "The high level of fibrinogen showed he was not right and suggests he was over the top."

Before the blood test results had come through Generous had been given another piece of work to see whether it was worth running him in the Champion Stakes. He did not sparkle. His racing career was officially over.

Maine continued: "Other than that he was one of the healthiest horses I have ever dealt with. A very sound horse, I expect if you X-rayed his joints now there would be no deterioration from the day he walked into the yard, he was that sort of horse."

Generous will be remembered as the horse who put Alan Munro on the map. "To say I was extremely lucky to ride him at this stage of my career is an understatement. Without Generous I wouldn't be half the person I am today. He had so few complications and a wonderful nature, what more could I have asked for? He was one of those horses that did not just want to win; when he got to the front he was not thinking that he had done enough, no, he was thinking how far can I beat this lot. I will be very, very lucky to sit on another of his like."

Generous helped Paul Cole to his first Trainers' Championship. "If I had a chance to retrain him for the Arc again I would do it exactly the same," he says. "I just think the race came a week too late. But he was a fantastic horse to train. I certainly wouldn't mind another Generous."

BREEDING APPENDIX

By Tony Morris

AFTER two centuries of study by the supposedly ablest brains, the pages of the General Stud Book have yet to yield a more meaningful formula for breeding success than "mate the best with the best and hope for the best". What is more, it would be difficult for as many as two alleged "experts" to agree on just how to define what was best.

The trouble with most pedigree analysis is that we tend to confine it to the backgrounds of good horses; we don't research the pedigree of failed platers, and we don't even bother with those of quite serviceable animals, who pay their way and provide their share of fun. We restrict our interest to the tiny minority who are the most successful, and when we conduct our research, there is hindsight to cloud our judgement.

With hindsight to help us, Generous is 'obviously' a very well-bred horse. By a winner of the Prix du Jockey-Club and the Benson & Hedges Gold Cup out of mare whose sire won an American Classic and whose dam was both dam and grand-dam of outstanding international racemares, he could seem to qualify by right as one of those produced according to that formula of mating "the best with the best". In fact, there are less flattering – and equally justifiable – ways of reading the pedigree, and it would hardly be stretching a point to suggest that "hoping for the best" was the closest approach to science in the match between his sire and dam.

In all honesty, there was no reason to expect a champion as the outcome to that mating. Caerleon covered around 200 mares in his first three seasons at stud, many of them regally-bred and apparently every bit as entitled to produce high-class performers as Doff the Derby. The record showed that Caerleon could get winners, plenty of them and some with appreciable class, but it also appeared to indicate that he was not capable of getting horses of his own racing calibre. That is a common enough phenomenon in the history of the breed; while it is generally true (in the northern hemisphere, at least) that most of the prominent sires come from the ranks of prominent runners, most prominent runners do not become prominent sires. Few horses make a habit of getting progeny as good as themselves, and it is a rare one indeed who manages to sire stock which surpass him.

All the evidence of Caerleon's first three seasons at stud pointed to his being some way short of a top-class sire. Nobody could say that he had lacked opportunities, in terms of either quality or quantity of his mares, but there seemed to be definite limits to the calibre of his progeny; he could get horses of first-rate ability in Italy, but horses of only second-rate merit in the more competitive racing regimes of Britain, France and Ireland. Because he had been decidedly a first-rate performer in the best company himself, he had to be regarded as something of a disappointment.

For all that, the Classic winner who fails to sire a profusion of Classic-winning stock is not necessarily a failure. Caerleon quickly established that he had a notable role to play, turning out a formidable array of above-average winners – in a variety of shapes and sizes and over a variety of distances. He got precocious types, like the Queen Mary Stakes winner Gloriella, and he got others, like the Park Hill Stakes heroine Casey, who got better as time wore on and distances opened out. Stayer

Casey and sprinter Caerwent (who won the National Stakes) were both out of daughters of Habitat.

Make no mistake, Caerleon had his uses. Any horse with the capacity to get such an abundance of winners deserved respect, and he might even be excused the lack of any kind of pattern about their pedigrees and performances. There was, as it were, a kind of consistency about their inconsistency. But there was another important element which bore on Caerleon's record, in that he had stood in those first three seasons at the inflated stud fee of Ir £80,000 gns. A horse's entitlement to respect for reliability in getting his quota of above-average performers must be qualified when the charge for his services is on a level which promises potential runners of Classic calibre.

Inevitably, Caerleon's fee was substantially reduced in his fourth season, by which time a majority of his auctioned stock had failed to recover the nomination price. The profusion of winners counted for less than the absence of a runner of really high class when a substantial majority of auction yearlings from the fourth crop, conceived at a reduced fee, failed to make money for their vendors. His services still seemed to be valued too highly for the quality of the stock he was able to produce; a season (1988) as champion sire, largely brought about by the victory in an Irish restricted race of immense value by a two-year-old of no great distinction in Corwyn Bay, could not halt Caerleon's commercial slide.

Yet while that mass of evidence, hinting at Caerleon's overall inadequacies, built up, there came from that fourth crop a colt who bucked the trend, and kept bucking it. As a group they may have lacked commercial appeal, but the sire's son from Doff the Derby made money for his breeder, David Nagle, when he was sold for Ir £80,000 gns as a foal; for his first buyer, Hamish Alexander, when he was re-sold for Ir £200,000 gns as a yearling; and for the man who raced him, Prince Fahd Salman, who picked up one seven-figure sum from his earnings at the track, and a second when he disposed of 15 shares for £175,000 apiece.

The suspicion that Caerleon would never get a horse of his own racing class was ultimately rendered ridiculous by the exploits of his impeccable chestnut son in the summer of 1991. But one Generous will not transform his reputation into that of a super-sire at this stage, and the somewhat fortuitous Prix de Diane victory of another fourth-crop product, Caerlina, could scarcely be expected to make much difference. The overwhelming weight of evidence still insists that Caerleon is not a great sire, and the belief, even the certainty, that Generous is a great racehorse need not contradict that view. Nobody would presume to suggest that either Tenerani (who got Ribot) or Dan Cupid (who got Sea-Bird) was a great sire.

It is tempting to form the opinion that Generous, by so wide a margin the best of his sire's runners, must owe most of his merit to his dame. And it is not altogether illogical to argue that point, although Doff the Derby, far from boasting a brilliant racing record, was actually never trained and was covered for the first time as a two-year-old.

The point is that whereas, generally speaking, we do not grant places at stud to colts who have not established their racing merit, there is no such requirement for fillies. We are happy to forgive the females, whatever the reason for their lack of form, and there are countless examples to indicate that such judgement is not misplaced. Generous is a typical product of the northern hemisphere breed, in that he has a sire who showed high-class form and a dam who did not. But we do not ignore or belittle the dam's contribution; we acknowledge that genetically each parent has the same potential to influence the offspring of a mating between them, and we recognise that factors which we fail to notice in one generation may yet be present, and transmitted to the next.

181

As far as fulfilling the notion that Thoroughbreds are supposed to race is concerned, Doff the Derby was a duffer. But her background had seemed to promise her toughness and a measure of class, so it was reasonable to reckon that, whatever the cause of her unsoundness, there was a strong chance that she owned valuable qualities and might transmit them, although she had been unable to express them herself.

Most authorities would reckon that Doff the Derby's sire, Master Derby, is the one real blot on the Generous pedigree. If that judgement seems harsh in view of Master Derby's eminently commendable record of 16 wins (including the Classic Preakness Stakes) from 33 starts, and harsher still on account of the Kentucky Derby victory of Dust Commander, Master Derby's sire, it is more understandable on the basis of stud performance. Master Derby was actually a rather better runner than his second-rate pedigree prophesied, and the same was true of Dust Commander.

There were high points in the stud career of Dust Commander (part of which was spent in Japan), but ultimately he would be remembered for Master Derby and nothing else. Master Derby, in his turn, got a lot of better-than-ordinary performers, but even a keen fan of American racing would be hard pressed to name two or three of real class. Both horses "out-ran their pedigrees" at the track, and reverted to type in their stallion careers.

Much the better half of the mating which produced Doff the Derby was the dam, Margarethen, a daughter of 1952 Derby winner Tulyar out of a mare by the exceptional international sire Nasrullah (which made her inbred to unbeaten racing and stud celebrity Nearco). Margarethen was bred to be classy, and she was, with toughness to boot. She stood training for five seasons, had 64 starts and won 16 times, competing with, and often beating, many of the rest of the best mares in action on the New York circuit around the mid-sixties.

More significantly, the qualities Margarethen exhibited she also replicated in her offspring. Her daughter Trillion (by the outstanding two-year-old and excellent sire Hail to Reason) showed similar toughness while representing rather higher class; campaigned in Europe, she won seven times in Pattern company, including the Group 1 Prix Ganay, and she was twice placed in the Prix de l'Arc de Triomphe. Excursions to her native land brought her no additional victories, but nevertheless showed her in a favourable light; as a five-year-old she was placed second four times at Grade 1 level in open competition with males.

If Trillion could be described as an outstanding race-mare, as she surely might be, how should we refer to Triptych, her daughter by the excellent miler and top-ranking sire, Riverman? Triptych was not exactly invincible, but she competed with the best runners around in Europe for five consecutive seasons, she displayed the utmost class, gameness and consistency, she won a total of 12 Pattern races, among them an Irish 2,000 Guineas, a couple of Coronation Cups and two editions of the Champion Stakes. She represented a further advance on the form shown by her mother and her grandmother, and it was a tragedy when she succumbed to a freak accident in a Kentucky paddock, pregnant for the first time to a mating with the exceptional sire Mr Prospector.

In many respects it would seem that the best of Generous' pedigree is to be found in the bottom quarter, where proven merit seemed to be most reliably transmitted, at least until the mating with the indifferent Master Derby resulted in the unraced Doff the Derby. But we did not have to wait for Generous to come along before Doff the Derby's worth as a broodmare was apparent; her previous foal was the filly Wedding Bouquet, who won in

Pattern company in Ireland and went on to register a Graded Stakes victory in America.

Interestingly, and possibly significantly, Wedding Bouquet was by Kings Lake, which gave her an even closer link with Generous. Like Caerleon, Kings Lake was a Classic-winning son of Nijinsky, and, like him again, something of an under-achiever at stud, considering the excellent opportunities afforded him in his early years as a stallion. Kings Lake had as much, if not more, pedigree as Caerleon, but he squandered his chances to such an extent that he was eventually despatched to Germany. It says something for Doff the Derby that she could produce one of the few worthwhile products of Kings Lake, as well as by far the most important performer by Caerleon.

Of course, we shall never know what made Generous a racehorse of the highest calibre, and by looking for the reasons in his pedigree we could easily be, as it were, barking up the wrong family tree. Like most exceptional runners, he is better than his pedigree, and anything but typical, in terms of racing merit, of the stock associated with his sire. One of the most fascinating prospects of the years to come will be that of observing Generous' progress at stud. Will that fortuitous blend of genes, responsible for this racehorse of exceptional merit, be transmitted faithfully to the next generation? It is anybody's guess, for the past is an uncertain guide in such matters.

GENEROUS (IRE)
CHESNUT COLT 1988

Sire: CAERLEON (USA)
(b. 1980)

- NIJINSKY
  - NORTHERN DANCER
  - FLAMING PAGE
- FORESEER
  - ROUND TABLE
  - REGAL GLEAM

Dam: DOFF THE DERBY (USA)
(b. 1981)

- MASTER DERBY
  - DUST COMMANDER
  - MADAM JERRY
- MARGARETHEN
  - TULYAR
  - RUSS-MARIE

185

2nd May 1990
Ascot
Good to Firm
Garter Stakes (Graduation Race)
5f
Two yrs old
1st £7,245

1   Generous (IRE)   8–12   *T Quinn*
2   Les Animaux Nuages (FR)   9–04   *Pat Eddery*
3   Grey Rooster (USA)   9–04   *J Reid*
4   Sylva Honda   8–12   *M Roberts*

Also ran: South Crofty, Don't Give Up, 6 ran.
Distances: ½l, ½l, 1l
Betting: 1st, 6/1, 2nd, 4/1, 3rd 5/4F

19th June 1990
Royal Ascot
Good to Firm
Coventry Stakes (Group 3)
6f
Two yrs old
1st £24,368

1   Mac's Imp (USA)   8–13   *A Munro*
2   Generous (IRE)   8–13   *W Carson*
3   Bold Nephew   8–13   *R Cochrane*
4   Tinkins Wood   8–13   *S Cauthen*

Also ran: Big Blow, Jim's Wish (IRE), Hailsham (CAN),
          Foursingh, Soweto (IRE), Beloved Visitor (USA),
          Time For The Blues (IRE), Groombridge (USA),
          Fitahl (USA), 13 ran.
Distances: 2l, 1½l, 4l
Betting: 1st 2/1F, 2nd 8/1, 3rd 12/1

186

2nd August 1990
Goodwood
Good to Firm
Lanson Champagne Vintage Stakes (Group 3)
7f
Two yrs old
1st £18,494

1　Mukaddamah (USA)　*W Carson*
2　Flying Brave　8–11　*S Cauthen*
3　Generous (IRE)　8–11　*T Quinn*
4　Andrath (IRE)　8–11　*M Roberts*

Also ran: Corrupt (USA), Half A Tick (USA), 6 ran.
Distances: 1½l, 3l, 1½l
Betting: 1st 7/4F, 2nd 7/1, 3rd 2/1

19th August 1990
Deauville, France
Good to Soft
Prix Morny Agence Francaise (Group 1)
6f
Two yrs old
1st £107,181

1　Hector Protector (USA)　8–11　*F Head*
2　Divine Danse　8–08　*G. Guignard*
3　Acteur Francais (USA)　8–11　*C Asmussen*
4　Polemic (USA)　8–08　*Pat Eddery*

Also ran: Crack Regiment (USA), Dominion Gold (GB), Once
in My Life (IRE), Line Engaged (USA), Platinum
Pleasure (USA), Generous (IRE), The Perfect Life
(IRE), Tuned Audition (GB), 12 ran.
Distances: 1½l, 1½l, 3/4l
Betting: 1st 16/10F, 2nd 107/10, 3rd 28/10 – Pari-Mutuel Odds

18th September 1990
Sandown
Good
Reference Point Stakes
1m
Two yrs old
1st £4,265

1   Generous (IRE)   9–04   *T Quinn*
2   Rahdari (IRE)   8–09   *W R Swinburn*
3   Tapatch (IRE)   9–04   *Pat Eddery*
4   Battlers Green (IRE)   8–12   *J Williams*

4 ran
Distances: 1½l, 3l, 10l
Betting: 1st EvensF, 2nd 100/30, 3rd 5/2

19th October 1990
Newmarket
Good
Three Chimneys Dewhurst Stakes (Group 1)
7f
Two yrs old
1st £117,609

1   Generous (IRE)   9–00   *T Quinn*
2   Bog Trotter (USA)   9–00   *N Day*
3   Surrealist (IRE)   9–00   *L Piggott*
4   Mujtahid (USA)   9–00   *W Carson*

Also ran: Stark South (USA), Anjiz (USA), Kohinoor (IRE),
        Sedair, 8 ran.
Distances; 3/4l, 2½l, 2l
Betting; 1st 50/1, 2nd 8/1, 3rd 16/1

4th May 1991

Newmarket

Good

The General Accident 2,000 Guineas Stakes

(Group 1)

1m

Three yrs old

1st £107,994

1 Mystiko (USA)   9–00   *M Roberts*
2 Lycius (USA)   9–00   *S Cauthen*
3 Ganges (USA)   9–00   *F Head*
4 Generous (IRE)   9–00   *T Quinn*

Also ran: Mukaddamah (USA), Desert Sun, Flying Brave, Hokusai (USA), Malvernico (IRE), Shalford (IRE), Marju (IRE), Bog Trotter (USA), Mujaazif (USA), Junk Bond, 14 ran.

Distances: Hd, 6l, 2½l

Betting; 1st 13/2, 2nd 16/1, 3rd 16/1

5th June 1991

Epsom

Good to Firm

Ever Ready Derby (Group 1)

1m 4f 10yds

Three yrs old

1st £355,000

1 Generous (IRE)   9–00   *A Munro*
2 Marju (IRE)   9–00   *W Carson*
3 Star Of Gdansk (USA)   9–00   *C Roche*
4 Hector Protector (USA)   9–00   *F Head*

Also ran: Hundra (USA), Corrupt (USA), Hokusai (USA), Hailsham (CAN), Toulon, Mystiko (USA), Environment Friend, Arokat (USA), Mujaazif (USA), 13 ran.

Distances: 5l, 7l, ½l

Betting: 1st 9/1, 2nd 14/1, 3rd 14/1

30th June 1991

The Curragh, Ireland

Yielding

Budweiser Irish Derby (Group 1)

1m 4f

Three yrs old

Ir £366,500

1   Generous (IRE)   9–00   *A Munro*
2   Suave Dancer (USA)   9–00   *W R Swinburn*
3   Star of Gdansk (USA)   9–00   *C Roche*
4   Sportsworld (USA)   9–00   *L Piggott*

Also ran: Nordic Admirer (IRE), Barry's Run (IRE), 6 ran
Distances: 3l, 8l, 2l
Betting: 1st EvensF, 2nd 9/4, 3rd 12/1

27th July 1991

Ascot

Good

King George VI And The Queen Elizabeth Diamond Stakes (Group 1)

1m 4f

Three yrs old and upwards

1st £276,480

1   Generous (IRE) 3   8–09   *A Munro*
2   Sanglamore (USA) 4   9–07   *Pat Eddery*
3   Rock Hopper 4   9–07   *B Raymond*
4   Terimon 5   9–07   *M Roberts*

Also ran: Sapience, Saddlers' Hall (IRE), Luchiroverte (IRE), Tiger Flower, Hailsham (CAN), 9 ran.
Distance: 7l, 1l, 1½l
Betting: 1st 4/6F, 2nd 7/1, 3rd 8/1

6th October 1991
Longchamp, France
Good to Soft
CIGA Prix de L'Arc de Triomphe (Group 1)
1m 4f
Three yrs old and upwards
1st £509,165

1 Suave Dancer (USA) 3   8–11   *C Asmussen*
2 Magic Night (FR) 3   8–08   *A Badel*
3 Pistolet Bleu (IRE) 3   8–11   *D Boeuf*
4 Toulon 3   8–11   *Pat Eddery*

Also ran: Pigeon Voyageur (IRE), In The Groove, Quest For
        Fame, Generous (IRE), El Senor (USA), Shamahir,
        Miss Alleged (USA), Art Bleu, Jet Ski Lady (USA),
        Snurge (IRE), 14 ran
Distances: 2l, 1l, 3l
Betting: 1st 37/10, 2nd 102/10, 3rd 68/10 – Pari-Mutuel Odds